Colin's
Big
Thing

Colin's
Big
Thing

A Sequence

Bruce Serafin

Ekstasis  Editions

National Library of Canada Cataloguing in Publication

Serafin, Bruce
    Colin's big thing : a sequence / Bruce Serafin.

ISBN 1-894800-26-5

    I.†Title.

PS8587.E695C64 2003   C814'.6   C2003-906279-1

Acknowledgements: The author thanks the Canada Council and Richard Olafson.

Published in 2004 by:
Ekstasis Editions Canada Ltd.   Ekstasis Editions
Box 8474, Main Postal Outlet   Box 571
Victoria, B.C. V8W 3S1   Banff, Alberta T0L 0C0

THE CANADA COUNCIL | LE CONSEIL DES ARTS
FOR THE ARTS | DU CANADA
SINCE 1957 | DEPUIS 1957

BRITISH
COLUMBIA
ARTS COUNCIL
Supported by the Province of British Columbia

Colin's Big Thing has been published with the assistance of grants from the Canada Council for the Arts and the British Columbia Arts Board administered by the Cultural Services Branch of British Columbia.

for Sharon
then and now

Around here, history, like most things, was makeshift, amateur, in comparison to what we knew was back east. Like a plywood cafe in Kispiox as opposed to a wise-crack deli in New York.

George Bowering

Contents

I

1. Mosquitoes

I

On September 6, 1961, my mom, me, my brother Mike, my sisters Annette and Marie-Claire and baby Paul all catch a train to the coast.

My dad's gone ahead. When we arrive, running throught the echoing train station with its hard floors, he meets us and leads us outside to a new white Ford station wagon with a third seat in the back.

The car thrills us. But even better is Vancouver. Nothing has prepared us for what we see. As we drive slowly along Pacific Avenue toward Stanley Park, passing futuristic buildings whose entire fronts seem to be made of glass, my mom puts a hand to her mouth with delight.

"Dear, this is so *beautiful!*"

"You like it," my dad says.

"I love it! I had no *idea* it would look like this. And the ocean, my word."

The Pacific Ocean we can only absorb slowly. It keeps being there as we drive, a line of light right beside the smooth black asphalt road. Our delight grows and grows. In Stanley Park the huge cedars—so differently scaled than what we're used to—make us hush as we drive slowly past them. A paved road goes right through one of these enormous trees, and when we see that it's as if our own size changes.

My dad drives onto Lion's Gate Bridge. We stare at the arcs of its suspension cables and the water wrinkling far below. And now something occurs that years later I'll linger over. Mike, my brother, has been pushing a little stone into his nose, something he does when he's anxious. I jeer at him; he starts to cry. When my mom notices his tears in the rear view mirror and turns around and asks him what's wrong, he puts his hand up over his nose and says, "I dunno."

A moment later I say, "Where we gonna stay, Dad?"

"The Alpine Court Motel. In North Vancouver."

"Are we gonna be there long?"

"Not too long."

And in the Alpine Court Motel the world in which my brother and sisters and I have been as close as puppies alters for good: for the first time we encounter TV. While our parents take baby Paul out for a look around, Mike and Annette and Marie-Claire and I sit on the floor in front of the set. *The Howdy Doody Show* ends: the first show we see from beginning to end is *Funorama*, an hour-long sequence of cartoons on Channel 12 from Bellingham. The sight, at the start of the show, of Popeye and Sweet Pea and Olive Oyl running around the show's titles fills Annette—gentle Annette—with such a sense of pleasure that she laughs out loud. We watch, fixated; and right from those first minutes of watching we begin to enter separate worlds and to develop the most important skill in our new life: consumption.

One Saturday a little less than a year later, drifting down Lonsdale, I notice a sign in the window of a place named Slan

Books. The sign says:

Science Fiction Paperbacks
20-25 Cents
Exchange Your Used Books

I have a brainwave. In my pocket I carry fifty cents allowance, enough to go to a movie and buy some candy; now, using that allowance, I buy two books. Next Saturday I exchange them for two other books, and buy two new ones. Soon, in this gloomy store smelling of paper in which I immediately feel at home, I'm exchanging ten or more books at a time and spending four or five afternoons a week.

On one of these afternoons, fiddling with the front of my pants in my excitement, I stare for the dozenth time at an envelope holding a letter I've just received. It's from Ginny Yeats. I've loved Ginny since I was seven. As I'm staring at the envelope that holds her letter, Alex McLean, the store's owner, walks over to see what I'm doing.

He looks at the envelope with me. I don't really mind. Alex is a fat, very short man with bright red cheeks who as usual is wearing jeans with the cuffs turned up so much they make him look like a clown. He isn't a clown, though. He invariably talks to me in a cynical, blasphemous way which pulls me toward him and makes me interested in him even though his words often sting me. He talks to me as if I'm also an adult.

On the envelope's upper left corner, Ginny's name and Hinton Alberta address are written in a round child's hand. An eight-cent stamp has been taped to the upper right corner. In the middle of the envelope my name and address are printed in big letters that slope up. Inside is a folded, lined sheet of pale blue paper, with lines of writing on it in the same round, upward-sloping child's hand.

I take the sheet out. It reads:

> *Do you still ride horses? I still do. We have a new horse named Bonnie. Do you still do high jump? All the kids in town have been picking pine cones this year. They are giving us a dollar for every sack. Do you remember when we used to pick pine cones together and then ride our horses home?*

I do. I remember we picked the cones on the other side of the highway, out from under the hill. I remember we picked the sappy tight new ones, putting them into bags supplied by the mill, and I remember the cones' green smell, the burlap smell of our bags and how Ginny's shoulder brushed mine as we walked between the trees toward her dad's horses.

When I once more finish the letter and fold it and put it back in its envelope, Alex says: "This is the girl you love."

I blush. "I dunno."

"Sure you know. You're lucky, too. You'll never have a love again so pure and intense."

My face is on fire. I look at him, then away.

"You think I'm kidding?" he says. "I mean it."

That evening, on an especially big sheet of yellow paper that was used for packing, I start writing Ginny the longest piece of writing I've ever written.

Her letter has filled me with emotion. As if I was old, I remember the secret world we knew when I still lived in Hinton, where next to the concrete base of our house daddy longlegs sat beside little sacs of eggs, where under the concrete steps (in the dark, on the cold dust) black spiders crawled, and where we banged sticks against the big stinking metal cans by the backyard fences where all of us in Hinton burned our garbage.

I'm in a different world now. It rains here. The bush is like jungle and you can't go into it. Kids almost never play in the streets, so I don't know how to make friends. Still, caught up in the happiness of writing to Ginny, the words flow faster than I can keep up. I write about the North Vancouver buses, about the TV shows "Seahunt" and "The Aquanauts," about how kids go snorkeling in the little lake up in the bush, about the frogs I found in a pond behind Danny Kerr's house and about the rowboat Keith Green and I discovered under the Second Narrows Bridge. Then I rewrite all this in my best handwriting on regular letter paper. That second time I hold the pen so tightly my fingers hurt.

Four months later Alex catches me crying.

"What's wrong?"

"Nothing's wrong."

"But you're crying."

What can I tell him? I stare at the shelves of books, hardly seeing them through the blur of tears. Mortification reddens my face.

"Having trouble at home?"

I shrug.

"Of course you are. Why don't you admit it?"

I look at him, already angry.

"How do you know that?" I say.

"It's obvious. Marriage and families should be abolished. There are no greater breeding grounds for unhappiness and power politics. You know what?" He stops shelving books and turns and faces me. This is a sign he's going to try to get me upset. And he does: "What you really want to do right now is kill your father and have sexual intercourse with your mother."

"I do not!"

We start to argue; and right away he gets my story out of me.

That morning, seething with frustration from an hour spent trying to fix our new clothes dryer, my dad nearly stepped on

Mike, who was lying on the kitchen floor reading *The Vancouver Sun*. We're supposed to keep the *Sun* neat until my dad finishes with it. But the pages are spread everywhere. My dad grabs Mike by the back of his shirt and yanks him into the air. He shouts, "Look what you did to the paper!"

I scream, "Leave Mike alone!"

My dad stares at me. "You mind your own goddamn business!"

My mom says, "By god, don't you talk to Bruce like that! Just because you're too bloody impatient to fix the dryer you take it out on the kids!"

"You want to fix the dryer?" My dad's eyes are bugged out of his head with anger. He flings the crescent wrench he's carrying so hard it flies across the kitchen floor and bangs into the counter, shocking us. "You want to fix it? You go ahead! You fix it!"

My mom's beautiful face flushes with anger. Her eyes fill. She picks up the crescent wrench and walks over to my dad and hits his arm with it.

He shouts, "You ignorant cow!"

I shout, "Don't swear at mom!"

With Mike and my sisters white-faced with fear, and full of the misery that a child feels when his family has come undone, I run out the door and walk and run all the way to Alex's store.

Now I expect sympathy. But Alex surprises me. He says, "Don't be so bloody sensitive."

"Why do you say that?"

"You're parents are having a hard time too. You've got to be tougher and support them."

"But my dad is mean to my mom!"

"All the time? Every day?"

"No."

"Then take it on the chin. Don't be such a softie."

I decide I will try to be tougher. I walk home, feeling older than I did before.

Then my mom becomes pregnant again. Within weeks my dad loses the job that's taken him over the Lion's Gate bridge five days a week; and in the fall we move to Allenby Landing 120 miles up the coast. When we arrive, driving off the second ferry, we run into fog.

"This is neat," Annette says.

"Jeez, you can hardly see," Marie-Claire says.

"I never seen anything like *this*," Mike says.

Then we all look out the car windows in silence.

We move in October. Immediately I start going to Baden Powell Secondary in Port Timshan. The school bus that takes us to Timshan parks on the highway at the bottom of the hill. One foggy morning in January when I run down the hill, afraid as usual I might miss the bus, I see Jill, a girl I've become friends with, standing on the edge of a crowd of kids. She's twelve, my age, a girl with black hair and taunting black eyes, one of the swarm of kids aged from about eight to to fourteen that I now play with on the beach down by the Oceanside Hotel.

When we play tag, Jill lets my hand brush her breasts. Now she walks up to me, close, less than a foot away, and looks at me with her taunting eyes. My heart pounds.

"There's gonna be a fight."

"Who's fighting?"

" Rocky and another kid."

I inch into the crowd. Rocky, who's named after Rocky Marciano and who's one of the half-dozen or so boys in town who practice boxing, stands facing an older boy of about sixteen whose name I don't know. Rocky is impassive. The older boy already has his fists up and his eyes are white with fear.

All of us in the crowd standing around the two know how

the fight will go. Excitement grips us as would the excitement at a human sacrifice.

Somebody says, "Get him Rocky," and Rocky hits the older boy's nose so hard the cartilage breaks and blood spurts out. The boy screams. Rocky hits the older boy again in the same spot, so that the boy's nose becomes a pond of blood, and then hits him again quickly four or five times, smashing into his cheek and lips so that the lips burst open and we hear a crack. Then the boy falls and curls up on the ground in the fetal position, blood spurting from his nose and lips and from around his eyes.

His face is wrecked. He's whimpering, crying. Nobody bends down to help him. Instead, almost taking turns, we look at him impassively and walk from behind the bus up to the front and then up the steps, each of us walking past the bus driver who's been sitting at the wheel not noticing what's going on, or not caring, or maybe just afraid to intervene.

That afternoon in math class six-foot-tall Clay McKay, a boy who's twice been held back, starts snickering at a joke his girlfriend Alice has made. Alice is sitting on his knee, her skirt nearly all the way up her legs. When Clay's snicker turns into a laugh, Miss Aldry—a heavy woman with huge breasts who's ignorant of the algebra she's supposed to teach us—shouts, "What are you doing! I told you!"

Clay sniggers. With his two hands he shifts Alice further up his leg so that her panties show and the full length of her thighs is exposed. The classroom fills with the smell of sex.

Aldry picks up the yardstick and walks over to where he sits. Watching her approach, Clay smiles. She raises her arm and hits him as hard as she can twice across the shoulders with the stick.

"*Did*n't I *tell* you?" she says.

It must hurt; but Clay only casually raises his hand. "Hey," he says, looking around and smiling. The class starts to laugh. Denise, a Native girl who has eyes shiny as mink fur, calls out to her boyfriend, "Hey Kelly, let me sit in your lap, maybe she'll hit you."

Rage seizes Aldry. She screams, "Shut up, you!" and walks over to Denise. She raises the yardstick. As she does so, one of her huge breasts flops out of her dress. It's brown, big as a football, its thumb-sized nipple swirled around with coarse black hairs. We stare at it. Clay giggles. Then we all start screaming, as overcome with hysterical laughter as if Aldry had inadvertantly shitted onto the floor.

II

"Bruce, what's going on? What is happening with your grades? *What* is happening with your *grades?*"

"I don't know."

"That's not much of a response," my dad says.

"Well, I *don't know.*"

In fact, my grades don't surprise me. I understand what's up, even if I couldn't put it into words.

Most of the teachers dislike "bright" students. They've adapted themselves to a milieu where pregnancies at sixteen are common and where fights in the hall often end with punches and blood. And having adapted themselves, even going so far as to curry the favour of the stronger kids, many of the teachers become angry if you show acuity in class. Maybe not consciously; but each year, by grade twelve, in that school of over 800 kids, fewer than twenty students remain.

I've become sullen and defensive. But I've also acclimatized myself; and in doing so I've become friends with Ronny Ballard.

Ronny is skinny and small; his dark eyes look flatly out from a thin, hard, contemptuous face; he's grown his fingernails into talons; he combs his Brylcreemed hair straight back from his narrow forehead so that it lies in a wedge on his thin neck; and he has a snaggle tooth. And with that snarling tooth and the fingernails and the flat black eyes, he bowls the other kids over. Little though he is, older boys follow his lead. Girls are fascinated by him. Passing a knot of kids in the hall, he'll say in a low voice: "Blood pools, murder rules." When we're with other people I watch him from a distance. There are aspects of him I can't imitate, only observe. His impassivity, for instance, his ability to be more tightly controlled than the other kids: that's beyond me.

But in Allenby we play together and his coolness becomes a fierce concentration that I respond to with a concentration of my own. During one of these sessions of playing, when we're making a little trap for bugs under the trailer in which Ronny and his dad and his younger brother Duggy live—it's up on blocks, high enough so you can crawl under it into a dark space that smells of earth—during one of these sessions, Duggy joins us, crawling under the trailer holding up a slice of bread heavily buttered with margarine.

"What're you doing?" he says.

"Fuck off," Ronny says.

"*You* fuck off."

"I told you to fuck off, so fuck off!" Ronny says.

"You fuck off."

"You want me to *hit* you? Huh?"

"Go ahead and hit me."

"I fucking will."

"Go ahead."

Ronny lunges forward and Duggy backs off, lifting the slice of bread to his mouth. As he does so I notice nearly a dozen crisscrossing white scars on his arm along with a couple of new scars on the back of his hand, covered with red scab.

After he's left, I say, "How come he's got all that on his arm? Those scars."

"That's my dad," Ronny says.

"Your dad?"

"Yeah. He hits him. With his belt. The belt buckle."

"He hits him on the arms?"

"He hits him on the *face*. And fucking Duggy puts his arms

up."

"Holy cow."

Yeah. Well, he'd never hit me. He knows I'd kill him."

"Would you?"

"Uh huh." Ronny nods.

"How?"

He keeps working on the trap. Then he looks up. "I'd wait till he was asleep," he says softly. "Real asleep. Then I'd put newspaper soaked in gas on his legs and up to his waist where he wouldn't notice. Then I'd set him on fire."

Ronny educates me. We read and re-read the stories of H. P. Lovecraft. In the Timshan drug store we steal not just bags of potato chips (dropping them quickly into each other's parka hoods) but also Dracula and Frankenstein models. Licking our thinnest brushes to make fine tips, we carefully paint the inside of Dracula's cape the same bloodred as his lips.

And then in late spring our education leads us to a comic book saturated with blood that's just appeared in the Timshan drug store. It's set in a terrible future. It tells the story of a group of creatures called "cyborgs," a mixture of man and machine who have eyes like small flashlights embedded in their heads and tubular plastic veins running over their bodies. They both hate humans and yearn to become them. The inking in these comics is spiderish and dark and their tone is cold, without a trace of the risible note that lightened the issues of *Tales From the Crypt* we read before then. And as soon as we see them, Ronny and I feel the shock induced by a truly new product of popular culture.

We don't know what excites us. All we know is that something's going on, something that's connected to the new songs on the radio like "Telstar" and "Sally Go Round the Roses." And Ronny, with his concentration on darkness, with his sexuality but especially with his sense of style, his sensitivity to all things new—Ronny to me comes to embody this amorphous change. He reads the comics obsessively; and sometimes, watching him on the swim float, thin and white in his tight white bathing suit with its built-in belt, surrounded as always by a gang of kids and bent over a new issue, sometimes it seems to me that *Ronny* is a cyborg, that he's entered a stylish, inhuman world that I'm excluded from.

"Where you going."

We're standing on the beach. It's raining out.

"Manitoba."

"Yeah, but *where* in Manitoba. *Fuck*," Ronny says.

"Pine Falls. It's where my relatives live. Okay?"

"You gonna wear that?" he asks.

"Wear what?"

"That hat."

"Why? Something wrong with it?"

"Did I say that?"

"No, you implied it."

"I didn't *imply* anything," he says.

The hat's a snap brim straw hat with a brown and white band; along with it I wear a reversible raincoat, dark brown on one side and creamy white on the other. The day we leave I turn the collar up.

When we pull into the sultry August heat of Pine Falls the raincoat's long gone. I've pulled the hatbrim down anxiously over my forehead.

We walk into Auntie Pauline's house. In the neat small living room, sprawled on the floor, the couch, the various chairs, their dark eyes bright, their arms and legs tanned, our relatives greet us.

"Oh my god Johnny and Sylvia!" Auntie Pauline rushes up to my mom and dad and hugs them. Then she turns to my brother. "And you too Mike! And Annette! And Marie-Claire! And little

Paul! and baby Louise! Oh my god! How big you all are! How you've grown! Oh Chriss is it ever good to see you! You were just babies when you left here and now I turn around and here you are!"

One of my nieces pushes her hair out of her eyes. Her cheeks are flushed with blood as if she's been blushing. She's wearing only only the flimsiest of clothes. She smiles at me. "Hi. I'm Aline."

For the next few days us kids move around like Bedouins among the houses of my mom's brothers and sisters. The disciplines of my family vanish; I stay up past midnight, and in the late mornings go out with Aline into the hot summer sun, watching her as she walks barefoot down the town's old sidewalks wearing only her bathing suit.

One particularly hot day we go to the town swimming pool. I'm wearing my hat and my tight striped bathing suit with a built-in belt that I think accents my muscles. We swim then lie out on our towels, face down, listening to the shouts of the kids in the pool and smelling the chlorine and feeling the water dry on our backs and the backs of our legs. Aline murmurs, "You think I'm pretty?"

"Yeah." My heart pounds. My mouth feels dry.

"Good."

She presses the side of her body against me. "I'm chilly."

She lies on top of me. I can feel her breasts on my back, feel the weight of her legs on mine. Instantly I get a hard-on that painfully fills up my tight bathing suit. I shift my hips so my erection can move up the suit's front. I can feel its hardness and how it's almost poking out.

Aline whispers in my ear, "This feels good eh." I can hear the smile in her voice.

"Yeah."

For a couple of minutes we lie there, intensely excited,

almost motionless. Occasionally Aline moves her legs on mine, or her upper body. When friends walk by she calls to them.

Then she says, "You wanna go in now?"

"Uh, I think I'll just stay here for a bit."

"Okay. I'm going for a swim."

I lie there face down in the heat, waiting for my erection to subside, glad that my bathing suit is wet so the stain won't show.

Driving home. On the outskirts of Lethbridge, my dad says: "Okay. We can go on through the Crow's Nest or we can go up to Hinton."

"Hinton."

"Let's go to Hinton!"

"My vote is for Hinton!"

We drive into town in the late afternoon. And it's odd: I discover I've forgotten the hill outside town on the other side of the railroad tracks. How strange that is. I stare at the hill's curving line. For over four years of my life I saw that line every morning, white with snow in winter, dark green the rest of the year. How could I forget it? I stare at the hill, trying to catch something just on the edge of my comprehension....

We're sitting in our motel room having breakfast. Everyone's talking at once. Marie-Claire shouts, "Okay, everybody, SHUT UP! What're we gonna do today, mom?"

"We're going on a picnic. Uncle Paul and Auntie Annette are gonna join us."

"When did *they* move here?"

"They moved here just after we did. Don't you remember? Your dad helped Uncle Paul get a job in the mill."

Three hours later we drive off the highway and get out. The campsite is set back in the bush, under a high bluff. It's immersed in aspen leaves like medals that tremble and reflect light all around. A fresh sweet wind blows in our faces. Excited by the wind, us kids run into the bush past yellow flowers, bright scarlet tiger lilies, pinkish-purple wild roses. Higher up we can see lodgepole pine. Everything stands out with crystal clarity, so that the rock bluffs, crewcutted with pines, seem to press slightly against the blue sky. Shouting and laughing, we run toward the campsite's picnic cabin, a log structure that has screens on it to keep off the mosquitoes.

There are no mosquitoes in Vancouver and Allenby Landing. I've forgotten them. But now I remember them and everything associated with them—the mosquito repellent, the summer screen doors. And with that, what I tried to comprehend the day before, staring at the hill—the sense of my childhood—floods me. I feel intensely happy; glad to have a subject to talk about with my dad, I say, "I forgot about the mosquitoes. Good thing we brought this repellent. It smells strong eh?"

"It is strong," my dad says. "I suppose you forgot about the mosquitoes because you were so little when you came here. You weren't really aware of them."

Auntie Annette laughs. "You grew up with mosquitoes. Even when you were a baby. They sure had them out on the farm eh, you remember, Paul?"

Uncle Paul nods. He's sitting beside my dad at the picnic table, both of them facing out. Uncle Paul has his arm around my dad. "Those mosquitoes in Powerview eh, John, when you were out in the bush? Boy oh boy, they'd cover you like a shirt."

My dad smiles. He's relaxed in a way I've never seen before; and as I watch, the two men, the table at which they sit, the bush around it and the nearby highway all become varnished with a kind of glamour. I'm seeing into another life. The world around us in all its clarity is one I've left and now have come back to.

That evening, still feeling a bit of the afternoon's excitement, I call up Ginny Yeats. The phone rings twice. Then I hear a voice that after a second I realize is Ginny's mom I feel confused. I haven't expected her. I blurt out, "Is Ginny there?"

"Yes, she is. Who may I say is calling?"

"It's Bruce. Bruce Serafin."

"Oh! Oh! We heard you and your family were in town. She'd love to talk to you! Ginny!"

I hear whispers; then I hear her voice.

"Hello?"

"Hi."

"Hi!" Ginny laughs, happily and nervously; I laugh.

"Are you just visiting?" she says. "Or are you back to stay?"

"I'm not sure. I think we're gonna be here a couple days."

"Oh, good." She laughs again, and again I laugh with her.

"It's strange to hear your voice!" she says. "Where you staying?"

"The Foothills Motel."

"What's it like?"

"It's okay. A bit of a hole. But I was wondering….Are you doing anything this evening?"

"No, I'm not doing anything. Just sitting in the back yard probably."

"Okay, good." My heart pounds. I lean forward, holding the phone to my ear. "I was wondering. Would you like to go see the movie?"

"I'd love to go see the movie!"

A half hour later, dressed in jeans and zip-up ankle boots and my hat, I knock on the Yeats's front door and not the back door I knocked on when I was small. After a moment the door opens. Ginny steps onto the porch.

"Hi," she says.

"Hi," I say.

I stare at her. And as we walk down the street toward the theatre, I keep looking at her. With each look I feel almost sick with excitement. Like me, Ginny has become a sexual being. It astonishes me, the transformation of the nine-year-old girl I last saw into this vivid, actual teenage girl walking beside me. Ginny's country girl face with its flushed cheeks lightly dusted with acne, her wide-set eyes (I remember their beauty from all those years before, and this persistence of her childhood self sharpens what I feel), her soft lips, her sun-bleached hair, her small breasts behind her shirt, the swell of her hips in her faded-pink shorts, her scabbed calf from a fall earlier that week (the scab long and dark on her tanned leg) and the frayed running shoes on her feet—all this change and growth bring something almost violent to her presence beside me.

To Kill a Mockingbird is playing in the theatre. The ticket seller's booth seems shabby. The concession stand seems small. But I remember them, just as I remember the slope of the dark, sticky floor, the dusty seats, the seatbacks I put my knees up against as a boy.

After the movie we walk out into the night holding hands. My excitement has turned into hot, concentrated happiness. The whole trip seems to have led to this. We walk away from town and across the tracks.

"What's Vancouver like?" Ginny says, and I'm off. Trying to keep my voice low, I say, "It's great. The BC flag is stupid, though. The Alberta flag looks way better. What's neat, though, is they got this dance show on TV and kids from high school go to it. You dance and they film you. I was on that a couple times."

"What kind of dances?"

"Jive, twist. You know, Chubby Checker, do the twist. And there were these gangs of guys there, from some of the high schools with switch blades. Which a lot of the kids in Vancouver have."

I tell her about Allenby. I tell her how Kelly Joe pounded a boy's head against a locker at school until the locker dripped blood. And I tell her about Ronny and how sometimes sitting in the dark under the trailer with him, we can hear his dad hitting his brother.

We walk across the highway. The moon lifts above the hill. The night floods with light; and as our shadows flow from our feet, I suddenly have a powerful sense that it all belongs to me—the highway behind us, the bush, the Athabasca River we're headed toward, Hinton, the Rocky Mountains, the coast: it's mine. Holding hands, we step down the highway bank. We walk into shadow, then out into the open. The air is sweet with pine; the moon shines on the ground at our feet. It's a summer night in Alberta.

2. "Are You Rural?"

I

When you're young, certain events seem to draw a line in your life between what preceded them and what comes later. Not long after we got back from Pine Falls, I ran into Jill. She had a piece of news. "Ronny's mom is a tramp. Don't you know that? She goes out with other men. My mom told me. She's disgusting. Just the sight of her makes me wanna puke."

I had seen her a few times already, Ronny's mom—a small woman with dark hair and a small face walking unsteadily on the highway with Ronny's dad. Ronny's dad was small too. He had broken fingernails that were black under the moons, and he wore shirts with the sleeves cut off. Ronny's mom wore a tight skirt that showed off her legs; and that, along with her air of vulnerability, had made me wonder what it would be like to lie naked in bed with her.

Neither parent was home when, on a cool Saturday night around ten p.m., while I was playing with Ronny over at the trailer, his brother Duggy stepped out the trailer door, jumped off the steps and landed hard on the battery-powered record player which at that moment was playing our favourite song, "Monster Mash."

We were sitting on the ground. Ronny stood up.

Duggy stared at him. "Didn't mean to." He put his hand over his mouth, deeply frightened.

"'Didn't mean to.'"

Ronny walked toward his brother.

"Watcha gonna do?" Duggy backed away.

"You'll see." Ronny walked up the steps into the trailer. A few seconds later he came back out holding a butcher knife.

"C'mere," he said.

"I don't wanna come there."

"C'mere."

"I don't wanna."

"'I don't wanna.'"

Ronny stepped toward him. And then, just as we threw our fishing knives at trees, Ronny threw the butcher knife straight at his brother. It stuck deep into Duggy's chest. Duggy stared at us, wide-eyed. Then he sat down; a moment later he fell over. His eyes were wide open. The knife was still sticking out of him.

"Oh shit. Look what I did," Ronny said.

I looked at him. His hands were holding the sides of his head.

We went over to Duggy and called his name. He didn't respond. I picked up his arm and tried to feel his pulse. I couldn't feel anything. His arm was limp. He stared sightlessly up.

I felt a surge of panic. "Ronny, I think we gotta call an ambulance."

"No, we're not gonna do anything."

I stood up. "We can't just leave him lying here. What do you mean? We gotta do *some*thing."

"No! We're not gonna *do any*thing!"

"Ronny, we gotta do something. We can't just stay here."

"No." Ronny looked at me. His eyes were flat. He turned and stared into the bush. Then, before I knew what had happened, almost while I was still looking at him, trying to think, he was gone, running down the dirt road away from the trailer, then onto the highway.

I ran after him. I shouted, "Ronny, stop!" He pulled ahead of me, running fast. Soon I couldn't see him in the dark. Fog was rising from off the ocean. The fog smell mixed with the smell of the mill. Gulping the night air and tasting blood in my throat, I tried to comprehend the enormity of what had happened. Finally I decided I would never catch him and started running home, running up the hill's first turn, the second, then up to our house.

Nearly retching, my breath coming from me in gasps, I told my dad what had happened.

"I think maybe he really hurt him. I don't know."

"Okay. Just sit. Try to catch your breath. I'm calling the police. And then I want you to talk to them."

Toward dawn the next day Ronny was found by the Port Timshan RCMP walking along the highway. Duggy had died almost instantly: the knife had gone through his heart.

All that Sunday I stayed home. Dread sat in the pit of my stomach. I thought the police would come. I waited for the phone to ring. I waited for neighbours to knock on the door. But nothing happened.

The next morning I walked with my stomach clenching and unclenching toward the crowd of kids waiting for the school bus. Again, except for a few stares, nothing.

Monday, Tuesday.

Then I heard about it. On Wednesday, at the side of the school by the soccer field, a gang of kids led by Darryl Chambers and Brent Demoyne surrounded me and began an interrogation.

"He stick the knife in him or'd he throw it?"

"He threw it."

"Oh yeah? How far'd he throw it?"

"Pretty far."

Contemptuously: "You were *there* then."

"Uh huh."

"Well, why didn't you stop him?"

"Yeah, why didn't you stop him?"

Angrily, almost whining: "I couldn't *stop* him."

"Did you help him?"

"No, I didn't help him!"

"I bet you did."

"Yeah, I bet you did."

Desperately: "I didn't help him!"

"I bet you sucked his blood eh."

"What?"

"Yeah, we know about Ronny sucking his blood."

Close to tears now: "Ronny didn't do that!"

"How do *you* know? *You* ran away!"

"Ronny didn't do that!"

"Yeah he did. That Ronny's a fucking devil kid."

"Yeah, we know about you two."

"Know what?" I was scared there was something.

"We know about you and your fucking Dracula dolls and him with that towel always around his neck. Fucking psycho."

"Weird asshole."

Nearly whispering, my self-control almost shattered: "He isn't weird." My eyes had filled. All I could think of was I didn't want the tears to spill over.

A couple of days later down at the beach: "Ronny has fangs. He sucked Duggy's blood."

"Jill, that's stupid! Where'd you hear that?"

"Well, I think he does have fangs."

"Jill, that's so stupid!"

"My mom thinks so too. She said that Ronny's mom is a witch and a whore and she should be put in jail right along with her son."

"That's *crazy.*"

"Yeah, well I think it's neat."

On Friday night the police came. They questioned me with my parents present. I answered as best I could, full of dread.

The next morning, sitting in the kitchen eating breakfast, we heard a knock at the door. Annette said, "I'll get it!" She stood up, and Marie-Claire stood up with her. Keyed up, we followed the girls to the door.

It was the scoutmaster, Bob Robinson.

"Well, come in, Bob," my mom said. "What is it?"

"Well. I was wondering if I could talk to your son."

"May I ask why?"

"I'd like to ask him some questions about Duggy."

My mom's face tightened. "What questions?'

"Well….I'm here I guess sort of as the town's representative. And we need to know what happened. Because we need to do something about that boy."

"Do what? Ronny, you mean?" my mom said quickly.

"He's going to get off, you know."

"And what do you think *should* happen to him?" My mom was staring at him now.

"Well. We think he should be locked up. And the key should be thrown away."

My mom kept staring at him. "Do you know how old Ronny is? Do you know anything about his background? He's just a *boy*!"

"Well, pardon me, but he's not just a boy. He murdered his brother."

34

"He didn't murder him," I said. "It was an accident."

The scoutmaster looked at me. "An accident eh?"

"He didn't murder him. That's stupid."

"Are you covering up something?"

"No."

"Did you and Ronny drink his blood?"

"No!"

"Okay, Bruce, that's fine," my dad said. He leaned toward the scoutmaster. "He's already talked to the police. So I think that's enough for now."

The scoutmaster looked at him. "Well, John, I just wanted to talk...."

"Well, it's enough."

My dad stared at him.

"Okay," the scoutmaster said. He held up his hands and nodded. "All right. I hear you."

My dad held the door open. The scoutmaster stepped through it.

"What did Bruce do?" Annette asked after the door had closed.

"I didn't do anything!" I felt close to tears.

"We know that," my mom said. "God, the nerve of that man. What a son of a bitch."

My dad looked angrily at my mom. "There's no point wasting your breath on ignorance."

"Well, I *know* that!" My mom started to cry, and unhappiness bit at all of us.

Many years later, my mom, still beautiful and vivacious in her late sixties, told me, "These were terrible days. Just terrible. Just like in Hinton. Those bloody bush towns. God, you wouldn't believe how ignorant the people were. I just *hated* it."

My mom sipped her coffee. "I tell you, the things they said

about you. I'm glad I never told you about that. They thought you helped Ronny. Remember Mrs Frisch? That horrible old woman? She came around one afternoon and said we should move away. I got so angry I was in *tears*. I could have *hit* her! And even now, every time I think about her I just feel the same rage. Even now!"

"What did dad think about all that?"

"Oh—" My mom looked away, hurt in her eyes.

An old wound. My dad would have expected my mom to deal with whatever came from the event. And she had. Unhappy, with six kids now, unsure of her position and thinking at times that she was about to skid over the edge, she had felt the full force of people's fear.

About two weeks after the knife was thrown, I saw Ronny's mom in the Oceanside Hotel. She was sitting with a man; and when she saw me she began to cry, the tears spilling down her cheeks.

Some time later I saw Ronny's dad walking toward me on the highway. I stepped off the road and ran into the bush. I was mortally afraid of him—afraid he would hit me or otherwise do damage to me for betraying his son.

And maybe I was right to think that. The postmortem revealed that Duggy had scars all over his body along with burn marks and other signs of trauma. Two of his ribs had been fractured.

When these facts came out, everything changed. In that world of darkness and ignorance, Ronny the vampire disappeared; in his place came Ronny the poor boy who had released his tortured brother into a better life. Within a month Ronny had ascended into the realm of legend where in places like Timshan and Allenby Landing boy criminals maybe still go when the police arrive. He had been taken to Brannen Lake, kids said (I also heard he had gone to stay with relatives), a place where boys went when they stole cars. You could write him there. And girls did, addressing letters to "Ronny Ballard, Brannen Lake, British Columbia."

Girls fell in love with his image. Some said they had kissed him. One girl said that she had the jacket he'd worn when he killed his brother. Denise, the Native girl in my class with the shining eyes, told me she'd had sex with Ronny. Another girl in my class, who was also named Ronnie, cut out the picture of him that was in the Baden Powell yearbook and put it in a locket.

People remembered his impassive white face. One lunch hour when a bunch of us went to the Timshan shopping mall to buy cokes and barbecue potato chips, a girl from Danny Creek pointed to the mall's red and blue lights. "Remember how they'd shine in his hair? He looked like a movie star." Somebody wrote his name in white paint on the big rock at the bottom of the Timshan hill.

And then gradually the Ronny story faded away.

I never saw him again. As the weeks passed, the stabbing of his brother started to seem like a mishap. When I thought of Ronny I rarely saw him throwing the knife. More often I remembered him earlier that Saturday night on the beach. He had walked out of the dark carrying his transistor, his towel draped over his neck, his white face showing the tight hauteur I had always admired. In fact, it was the impassivity of a damaged boy. He was ugly, really, with his bony forehead and snarling mouth; he had a thin, white, ugly face, an undernourished boy's face with flat eyes—to me, now, a poignant face. Jill was sitting on the beach. And with "You've Lost That Lovin' Feeling" coming from his radio, Ronny stood with us watching the waves lap against the shore.

Mist out on the water; all around us tall trees blacker than the night. At our backs the highway that spread the culture of the little port towns Jill and Ronny had grown up in. It was a hard culture, permeated with alcohol and blood and sex, the logging and pulp mill culture of BC's coast. And now we belonged to it.

The high tide that stood level with us stretched out black and mysterious into the dark. It seemed we could almost see our futures out there.

Two months later my family moved to West Vancouver.

II

A warm Monday on the last week in November. Overdressed in a new sweater, shirt, pants and shoes, I walked from our house on the edge of the British Properties through a warren of streets that snaked around the side of the mountain—streets hidden from each other by tall cedars and enormous homes.

I became lost. And in my new clothes I started to sweat. The sweat ran down my forehead and my armpits. By the time I arrived at Hollyburn Secondary I was late by about five minutes. I ran in a panic to the principal's office to get directions, then ran down the hall toward my home room.

The room was empty except for a man looking out the window. He turned to me, briefly smiled. "Well, here you are. You can come with me down to your first class and help us debate something."

The man—sad-looking when he stopped smiling, heavy, short, wearing a V-necked sweater over a shirt and tie—walked with me down the wide hall. We entered a spacious classroom filled with light. Up at the front a boy sitting on the teacher's desk was swinging legs that were crossed at the ankles.

He jumped off the desk. He wore jeans with patches on them, a denim shirt whose sleeves were rolled up and over the shirt a vest made of dirty sheepskin. His hair touched his ears.

He smiled. Gently, the words not harming me, he said, "Ah, the new boy."

From every corner of the room, curious eyes.

Turned partly to me, partly to the class at large, the teacher

39

said, "This is Bruce Serafin. He's our new student. You can sit there, Bruce—" he pointed—"behind Bill, and he'll fill you in— okay, Bill?—as things proceed."

I sat at my desk and Bill turned around. He murmured, "It isn't quite the Spanish Inquisition, but it's pretty close."

The teacher said, "Today we're picking on Don because in home room he won't stand up and recite the Lord's Prayer. Our Vice Principal Mr Dunley says that until he gets a note from his parents he *will* recite the Lord's Prayer or face staying in after school. Okay Don, you can go back to your seat." He waited until Don had sat down; then he turned slightly and addressed the class at large. "Should Don recite the Lord's Prayer with the rest of you?"

A tall boy at the back with a gentle horselike face said, "If he doesn't interfere with anybody else reciting it I don't see why he should have to."

"No proseletyzing, Don!" a girl with garish eyelashes said.

Don quickly said, "You mean a Unitarian lad like me can't do missionary work?"

A boy wearing a tie—he was smiling: his eyes were bright with laughter—said, "We all know Don is anti-establishment. I wouldn't expect anything less from him than this kind of grand-standing."

"Jack! You shock me!" Don said. "It's a point of principle. Hardly grandstanding."

The teacher—whom I would later learn was named Mr Taylor—held up a hand. "Okay. What's the argument why Don *should* recite the Lord's Prayer?"

"Because we all do it," the boy wearing the tie said. "Why else."

"That's pretty weak," the girl with the eyelashes said.

Mr Taylor said, "Well, I don't know. Convention is a pow-erful thing. Most of the things we do, we do because other people do them, don't you think?"

By lunchtime I had learned that the boys didn't hit each other. They made jokes. They used irony in their conversation.

That afternoon at phys ed we played soccer. Don Ross was a natural athete, running with grace and force. I loved soccer, and Don pulled me in, calling to me and passing me the ball when he could.

Afterward we squatted on the edge of the field, watching a fog roll in and eat the trees.

I said, "You guys are pretty good."

Don smiled. "Actually, we're not big on sports here. We have a rugby team that's fairly terrific but there's lots of other things if you're interested."

"What things?"

"Oh, we have a chess club, a UN club, electronics club. Let's see. Photography club. Math club."

"A math club?"

"Yeah, Bill Crepax, the guy you were sitting behind in Socials, right, he's a math genius. He started it."

"Maybe I'll go to that one."

"You like math?"

I nodded.

"Well, you and Bill'll get along then."

In January, as one of my electives, I chose art. The teacher, Mr. Hanson, a heavy-eyed, dark-haired man who wore dark shirts and dark ties, sat on the counter and muttered instructions to us. As soon as he could he took us all outside.

I hadn't had art in Baden Powell. There hadn't been an art class. But I loved it. I liked everything about it. I liked the brushes and charcoal sticks we used; I liked the airy room that smelled of paint and glue and solvents. And I liked the gang of girls that I met in that airy room.

In late January, when we first went outside to draw trees, we sat together on our jackets on the ground. I sat beside Nadine, whose skirt moved up as she drew and showed the long white stockings on her legs. We sketched the same tree and, while the other girls listened, we talked.

"Where're you from?" Nadine said briskly.

"Allenby Landing."

That's near Port Timshan, isn't it?"

"It is."

"Jacq here has a place there."

"Her own place?"

"Don't be naive. No, her parents."

"Not actually there," Jacqueline said. (All the girls in the group had one-syllable nicknames—Na and Pam and Jacq and Rhon and Char.) "It's on a nearby island. But I know Port Timshan."

"You like it?" I said.

"I love it. It's so rural."

"I guess."

"Are you rural?"

"I don't know."

"Don't shake your foot so much," Nadine said. "You make me nervous. I can't draw when I'm nervous."

"I'm sorry I make you nervous."

"Don't say I'm sorry!"

"Don't smile!" Jacq said.

"Don't breathe!" Char said.

One day, aware that I had now joined the photography club and was spending a lot of time in the darkroom, Don Ross said, "You should meet Alistair Fraser."

After classes that afternoon he introduced me to a silent boy opening his locker. Majestically rolling his "r"s, Don said,

"Alistair's our Cartier-Bresson."

"Bug off," Alistair said.

Don smiled and held up his hands and walked away.

"What kind of camera do you use?" Alistair asked me.

"A Kodak." I shrugged. "It's the school's—it's kind of old but they let me check it out because I fixed the film advance."

Alistair nodded. "I've got an old Ensign."

"Never heard of that."

"It's ancient. Square format." With a light sarcasm, he added, "I think Cartier-Bresson might have taken a few pictures with it."

"I don't know who he is."

He's a French guy. You probably figured that out. What kind of pictures do you take?"

"Oh—this and that….Doorways."

"Doorways are good. I like corridors myself. Linoleum floors."

By now we were walking down the hall together.

"I just moved here too," Alistair said. "How do you like Hollyburn?"

"I like it a lot."

"I do too," he said.

I looked at him. Reddish brown hair, pale eyes, unpolished black shoes, tan pants, a short-sleeved plaid shirt—clothes so plain he almost disappeared into the walls. But he had stood up to Don without even seeming to.

"Let's go to the smoke hole," he said.

It was a dip in the ground among cedars and thick bush, a kind of annex to a power line. Cigarette butts littered the ground and were especially thick near a cedar deadfall on which people could sit. The hydro pylon, pinned in its heavy concrete block (a block that was blackened here and there with cigarette ash and firecracker burns) rose up into the grey sky.

"You smoke?" Alistair said.

I nodded.

He held out an open pack of Players.

I didn't inhale yet. The cigarette tasted sweet, delicious.

While we were smoking, two boys walked up. One had a knobby, chinless face, brick-red as if he had just been embarrassed. The other was short and square-faced, with a jutting chin as if to make up for the first boy's lack, and gleaming black eyes.

"So the pig farmers are back," Alistair said.

"We saw a couple good ones."

"Tits out to here one of them."

"You're fucking sick."

"You're fucking sick. You're. Fucking. *Sick!*"

"Who's fucking sick?"

The three boys laughed and punched each other. The one with the brick-red face grinned at me. He held out his hand: "I'm Ned."

The short boy said: "I'm Andy."

"Andy the pig farmer," Alistair said.

"Fuck off! Fuck off! Ha ha ha!" Andy laughed harder and harder, bent over, holding himself. Then he straightened up. "Look what I learned today." He lit a cigarette; then he carefully blew one smoke ring through another and then a third through the second.

Alistair said, "Andy's in a good mood. He's been beating his meat."

Ned said, "Pronging his dong."

Feeling the spirit of things, I said, "Flicking his dick."

"So you're from Allenby Landing?" Alistair said.

"Yeah. But I grew up in Alberta. In Hinton."

"I'm from Estevan. Ned's from Moose Jaw. Andy's from Pinkie."

"Pinkie. I never heard of it."

"It's Little Pinkie," Andy said. "It's in Saskatchewan too, I'm proud to say."

"Land of wheat and cow farts," Alistair said.

"We got company," Ned said.

Three of the British Properties kids walked up to us.

"Hey Bill. Beat this," Andy said.

He blew three more smoke rings. Bill Crepax—who had an already Arabic beard so that even after he shaved his cheeks seemed covered in pepper—took the cigarette Andy offered. He held his cigarette between his thumb and finger, and I noticed that like Ronny he'd grown his fingernails into defiant talons.

Dave Phillips, a boy with red cheeks and curly hair, watched the rings of smoke fatten in the air then attenuate until they were no more than sketches. "Pretty good," he said. "But do you know how to spit."

He arched his back and leaned his arms back like a bird's wings. He leaned back his head. "Ghhhhhaaaaa," he said. And then he expectorated an enormous green wad of sputum to a distance that amazed the rest of us. Ken Wallace watched, smiling. He was the tall gentle boy with the horselike face whom I'd first seen in Mr. Taylor's class. He unselfconsciously sat on the ground with his legs out to the sides like a girl, and I realized, glancing at him, that he'd already become a friend.

Almost every day Don came to class wearing his dirty sheepskin vest and the jeans with patches. I thought he was poor. I was amazed that a poor boy attended Hollyburn Secondary and I felt sorry for him.

Then one morning in Social Studies I leaned over and whispered to Bill, "How come Don wears that vest?"

"What d'you mean?"

"That vest. And the jeans with patches. Is he poor?"

"No. He's rich. His dad's an airline pilot."

Don lived in a sort of small house or garage that was located next to the swimming pool of his parents' big home. It had a bedroom, a room to do homework in, a shower stall and a small kitchen.

One Saturday afternoon when he and I and Nadine and Pamela from the art class gang were out walking, Don said, "Let's go to my place and have an orgy."

Pamela looked at him. "You think so?"

"Absolutely."

"Good," Nadine said.

At Don's place I sniffed at the aromatic cedar siding in the shower stall and opened the door of the kitchen's gleaming half-sized fridge. Then we all sat on Don's big bed.

Don said, "Let's take off our clothes."

"But not our underwear," Pamela said.

Nadine, pulling off her jumper, said, "I'm virginal today. I'm wearing white."

"Me too," Pamela said, taking off her dress. Delicate in panties and bra, she slipped under the covers with apparent non-chalance.

I was nervous. I had big pimples on my back that I was ashamed of. But I took off my clothes nonetheless with the other kids.

And then, skinny, fourteen years old, wearing sagging underwear, I got under the covers.

Don and Nadine, Pamela and I lay side by side for a moment, not moving. Then Pamela kissed me. We put our arms around each other.

Pamela said, "Now what?"

"I don't know."

Of course I'd kissed a girl before. And in Pine Falls Aline had lain on top of me. But that had been hot and direct. What we were

46

doing now was sophisticated, cool. I'd moved to a new class of people.

Pamela whispered into my ear, "These sheets are cold."

I whispered back, "You think Don and Nadine are doing anything?"

"We could ask them."

"No, don't ask them."

After a moment Pamela said, "I don't know if I'm in the mood for sexual intercourse."

"Me either."

We kissed again.

And then we started to laugh. We were children still and we had failed in our orgy. But I'd noticed Pamela's silky white underwear and rounded hips, and from that afternoon I started thinking about her in a way I hadn't before.

"There's Don," Alistair said.

He was walking up Marine Drive with a friend whom we knew was from Highland Secondary and who wrote poetry about popsicles and elves. The friend had long hair and dark eyes and was wearing jeans with inserts in them from an older pair of jeans and an untucked baggy black shirt that buttoned tightly at the cuffs. Don was wearing a pair of black wool pants with yellow stripes down the side and a shirt patterned with black and white diamonds. His hair covered his ears.

This new look enchanted me. Everywhere now were hints or glimpses of it. Occasionally I saw a boy or girl on the street who had the new style and I wanted to follow them, just to keep them in my sight.

One afternoon in late August, getting ready for school, Don and Alistair and I walked down to Park Royal to buy our new wardrobes. It was sunny out, hot, and the lawns were crisp; but we could smell the salt breeze coming off the ocean. We were excited about the school year coming up and what we were going to do with the money we'd made that summer.

Park Royal was ready for us. Following our usual pattern, the three of us entered the mall from the Lions Gate Bridge side, close to the drug store, our first stop; and there, smelling the scent of soaps and lipsticks and candy that we associated with the girls floating by, we sat on the floor by the magazines and read *Tiger Beat* from front to back, meticulously studying every picture of Donovan and Bob Dylan.

"Maybe Eatons'll have one of those caps," Don said.

I nodded. "I'm gonna buy one if they do."

Next, a hot dog and an Orange Julius. And then the book store, where all three of us bought the latest *Talon*—it was a student literary magazine printed in North Vancouver that cost 25 cents—and flipped through Carl Sandberg's *Honey and Salt* and Yevgeny Yevtuskenko's *Babi Yar and Other Poems.*

Now we were ready. We strolled back down the mall and through the wide opening into Eatons. And there, in the unmistakable smell of new clothes, a paradise exclusively for bourgeois teenagers appeared before us: Dark blue pea coats with metal buttons, black leather sportscoats like the kind Bob Dylan wore on the cover of *Bringing it all Back Home,* purple or white shirts with puffy sleeves and Dr. Zhivago collars.

Don put on a Huck Finn cap and one of the black leather sportscoats. His arms folded, his hair hanging in his eyes under the black cordurey cap, he said, "What d'you think?"

I stared at him, dizzy at the transformation that had taken place. At that moment I knew that nothing in my life was ever going to be the same.

"Now this is a book you should read."

Don held it out. It was a thick white book with a red, white and blue print of the American flag on the cover.

"There's an amazing poem in here by Allen Ginsberg. It's called 'Howl.' You've got to read it." Don opened the book and showed me. "Just read it."

"Okay, I will." Already I was bent over the book.

One day when Alistair and I were listening to The Rolling Stones in his bedroom we heard a loud knock at the bedroom door.

Alistair said, "Come in."

His dad walked in. He stared at Alistair. With his voice barely controlled, he said: "What's this you're listening to—'I'll stick my knife right down your throat, and it hurts.' For Christ's sake, I didn't bring you up to listen to that kind of junk."

Alistair stared back at his dad. "What did you bring me up to do," he murmured.

"What?"

"Nothing. We're leaving." Alistair got up. "Come on. Let's get out of here."

III

One Saturday afternoon Alistair and Andy and I had bored ourselves walking through the British Properties looking for cigarette butts; now we decided to go to Ned's place.

When we got there Ned and his dad and mom were out on the lawn. Ned's dad was shouting at his mom. Ned was staring at his dad. When he saw us approach he walked over with his face blotchy red, smiling his soft smile. "I don't know what's with my dad right now," he said. "I just—I just—I just don't...."

"You bloody bitch," Ned's dad said. Then he started to slap Ned's mom. Slap. Slap. The slaps left red marks on her face.

Ned ran over to his dad. He said, "God, dad, please don't do that."

"*What*," his dad said. "Are you gonna stop me?" He punched Ned in the face. Ned fell. When he got up, tears were streaming down his face.

Andy walked over. He said, "Hey, don't hit Ned like that—"

Ned's dad turned and showed his teeth. He said, "Don't you tell me what I can do with my son! Mind your own fucking business! Get inside!" he said to his wife, turning back. And to Ned: "And you, you cunt, you're going to hear about this later. By god, I'm gonna strap you to within an inch of your life."

Later, walking toward Don's garage, Ned still had the painful grin on his face. His tears had left red marks on his cheeks.

That afternoon the five of us walk into the bush above the Properties. After a while we reach a dump which we like to stop at. There we take turns shooting Andy's .22 at tins. As one or the other of us carefully aims, we talk about our dads and ourselves.

"I don't hate him," Ned says. "I just feel I'm grotesque."

Alistair shoots and misses. He hands the rifle and the box of shells to Andy and says, "Ned, you're not grotesque. We're just in the pupal stage. And besides, it's your sense of being grotesque that makes you such a kind person. It helps you recognize other wounded or damaged people. Me, I don't feel that. I'm an egotist."

He continues, "But I know what you mean. When my parents have people over, they come over and ask about my hair, right, and I just go out."

"I wish I could do that," Ned says. "I just scuttle around. I'm like the phantom of the opera. I see one of my parents' friends and I can hardly lift my head."

Andy shoots: the tin goes flying. He grins and hands the rifle to Don. "It's our dads. We hardly ever see them. And so our relationship with them is fucked. And you know when we do see them, right, they're not like guys who have a role in our lives, like in the old days."

"That's right," Don says. He shoots and the tin spangs into the air. "That's it exactly. They're so touchily dominant they can't unbend or even just act freely before us. It's that anxiety about status that they have. And you know," he says, warming to his theme, "the anxiety in the British Properties has so many *consequences*. And one of the most important—and most untalked about—is that it make us boys ejaculate prematurely. Just like our dads."

Don has touched a nerve. Will we, when the time comes, be able to perform properly? Just the sight of a few inches of naked thigh gives us hard-ons.

"And also," he adds, "all this—all the anxiety in our houses about money—it all seems so awful to us because we're educated in a way that our parents aren't. It might seem pretentious to say so, but it's true that we know more than they do. I mean," Don continues, "they don't read Allen Ginsberg; they haven't had our education. They've worked hard to get us to where we are, but the tragedy is they don't *understand* where we are. I mean, can your parents listen to Bob Dylan? Even a great song like 'Masters of War': they don't get it. And so our own hatred of this middle-class milieu that we find ourself living in, right, it's just something they can't understand."

We all nod. He's spoken truth.

"We should start a magazine," Don says. We're sitting begging on the sidewalk in front of the Hudsons Bay. In front of us people stand lined up for the West Van buses; all around us, crowds of people walk in and out of the store. Pamela sits a few yards away, smoking, watching as Alistair snaps pictures of Don and Char and Ned and me. She thinks all this is silly, us coming down to Georgia Street to beg as if we were poor.

It was Don's idea. Alistair with his usual frankness has summed up the good and bad points: "Well, it'll feel romantic. It's fake though. Like Dylan himself. Middle class kid goes to New York, rides the El, bums money. Writes songs like Woody Guthrie."

"Yes, but romantic," Don says.

Alistair aims the camera at Pamela sitting against the wall of the Bay in her pea coat and black and white checked miniskirt and black stockings and high boots. She has her hair cut shaggily across her eyebrows in the new style so you can hardly see her face. Seeing the camera on her, she looks down at the sidewalk.

"Anyway," Don says, "we should start a magazine. We could put Alistair's pictures in it. And stories and poems."

"And drawings," Ned says. He likes to draw.

"Sure." Don says. "I'm positive we could get Freisen to help us. And Pam there works on the yearbook club so we could get her to produce it. With the yearbook people.

"Pam," he calls out, "We need you. Come here!"

Pamela stands up and takes a drag on her cigarette. Slowly, she walks over. And sits next to me on the curb. "Dear Pamela," Don says. "We want to start a magazine. What do you think?"

"Why ask me?"

"Because you're on the yearbook committee. You can produce it."

"It's not that simple."

"Sure it is," Char says. She looks at us, eyes dark with make-up under her Yves St-Laurent hair. "You just have to want to do it, that's all."

"I bite my tongue at you," Pamela says.

"I bite my tongue at you," Char says.

Don says: "We've just got to get Freisen on our side and we'll have no problems."

In Mr Freisen's English class that Monday we perform *Julius Ceasar*. Don is Marc Anthony. When his speech to the Romans arrives, he climbs onto his desk, slowly looks around and with a grandiloquent motion of his right arm intones:

"'Friends, Romans, countrymen, lend me your ears.'"

Andy reaches into his pocket and holds out a rubber ear cut from a halloween mask. "Will this do?"

When the play's finished, Don walks up to Mr Freisen and puts his arm around him. "Come on boys and girls, let's gather around our dear Mr. Freisen and let him know what we want."

We gather around.

"We want to start a magazine," Don says.

"A magazine. I assume you mean a literary magazine."

"A literary and artistic magazine."

Ned says, "With Alistair's pictures."

"We want to display our creative genius to the world," Don says.

"Well."

"Come on."

"Don, let me think about it."

"Come on."

After a minute Mr Freisen smiles. "Okay."

And so we start. Don and Alistair and Pamela are the bosses. Don for the literary part, Alistair for the photos and Pamela for the overall look. Part of Pamela's job is to come up with the cover design and the magazine's name.

In our English class next week we all gather near the front, some of us at our desks, others standing, others sitting on the counter along the windows. Alistair moves among us, his camera clicking away.

"Okay," Pamela says. "What do we want on the cover: photo or drawing."

"Photo."

"Drawing."

"What do you think, Alistair?"

He considers. "Drawing. Why not. More elegant that way. Photos inside. A photo on the cover's too rough."

Everybody nods.

"Okay, drawing," Pamela says. "Now what about the name of the magazine."

Nadine says: "Let's call it *Furious Wind*."

"Very nice," Mr Freisen says.

"Yeah, it is nice," Ned says. "But I was thinking…." He blushes, his face and throat on fire. "What about *The Ring*?"

Like the rest of us, Ned has read and re-read *The Lord of the Rings*. It's our favorite book, so much so that we see each other as characters in it: Strider and Gandalf and Frodo and Galadriel and Eowyn. I see Eowyn in Pamela or at least something of Eowyn.

We all see Don as Gandalf. But Alistair we can't pin down: he isn't quite Strider, but he isn't Frodo either. Andy, short and square-faced, is Gimli. Ned is Sam.

"Not *The Ring*, Ned. Too obvious," Bill Crepax says.

"How about *Firelight*," Andy says.

"No. Not *Firelight*."

Char says, "How about *Devil's Club*. A name of something local."

"Nothing local," Don says. "This is a literary magazine. Like *Talon*."

"*Talon* is such a great name."

"What about *Spear*?"

"*Spear* isn't bad."

"No, not *Spear*."

Mr Freisen sits on his desk, his legs crossed at the ankles, his pant legs neatly draped, his black socks and polished black shoes visible. He seems happy. He says, "Maybe I should start writing the names on the blackboard. When we reach a dozen names we can start crossing them off. And then when we have three left, we'll vote on them. Now be quick."

We are. After ten minutes, we have fifteen names on the blackboard, twelve of them cut through with careful slanting lines. The remaining names are: *The Misanthrope, Ambrosia* and *Firelight*.

We vote for *Firelight*.

Excellent," Andy says.

Now we get going.

Alistair wants to take pictures of the art class girls in the nude. Mr Freisen thinks about it for a minute. Finally he says, "Well, okay: but their private parts have to be covered. And you'd better be prepared for controversy."

And so Alistair uses up a roll of film photographing the girls in the art room surrounded by their drawings and sculptures. Underneath the photograph that he finally prints—three of his original pictures placed side-by-side—he writes a laconic, factual poem with a stanza devoted to each girl. The whole thing is far and away the best item in the magazine.

Don writes a story in the first person about winning the Nobel Prize for literature.

I take a photo of a doorway in shadow and use it to illustrate my story, which is called "Sonny's Blues." It's basically stolen from some writing I've read by James Baldwin. Ned does a drawing of us in suits of mail and calls it "On the fields of Pelenor." Pamela writes a terse story about a couple robbing a bank and dying out on the street.

The day arrives when we have to hand everything in. Mr Freisen is going to go over it, and then Pamela is going to get together with Nadine and start the design and production.

That night I get a phone call from Pamela. My heart pounds; she's never called me before.

"Pamela. Hi. How are you doing?"

"There's trouble."

"What's wrong?"

"Mr Freisen was going over the stuff. He recognized a story."

The blood pounds in my face.

"Whose story is it?"

"I don't know."

The next day at school Pamela says, "No, it wasn't yours. What did you think, it was you?"

"Who was it?"

"Mike Demott. He copied the entire story out."

"Do you know anything about him?"

She shakes her head.

Mike is in most of our classes but I've never talked to him. Only Bill knows anything about him. At the smokehole a few days later, he says: "After he got caught he tried to kill himself."

"Holy cow."

"Yeah, he tried to hang himself. He was in the closet on a chair, and he put a belt over the rail, right, and he kicked the chair out. No luck. And then, my dad said, his dad threatened to sue the school, but I don't know what's happening there."

Don says, "What does he look like? I can't place him."

Alistair says, "He's that guy sits in the back in social studies. He's got that really white face and that long nose. He looks like Rumpelstiltskin."

Jack, the boy with the tie and the laughing eyes, says, "Rumpelstiltskin?"

"Yeah, Rumpelstiltskin."

"Alistair, you're absurd sometimes."

A moment's silence. Then Andy says, "God, what'd he think he was doing, copying it word for word."

Jack says, "What a sorry maroon."

"D'you know anything about him?" Ned says.

"I know he moved here last year," Bill says. "He moved from Williams Lake. Before that he lived in Edmonton. His dad's a civil engineer. Alistair, give me a cigarette."

"Bill, you're a mooch," Andy says.

"I like being a mooch. Being a mooch suits me."

Andy nods. He's just thought of something. "Williams Lake. That's a neat place. I worked up there this summer. Ned, you been there."

"Just for a couple days."

"It's a wild place. All those Indians."

"What were you doing?" I ask.

"Flagman. Fifty bucks a day."

"How'd you get that?"

"My dad works in highways for the government. Anyway they got Indian squaws up there, man, I'm telling you it's just amazing."

We all step forward a bit. We want to hear about this.

"What kind of crudity are you going to tell us about now," Jack says.

His voice lower, almost whispering, Andy says, "Fuck, they're amazing. They'll put out for a buck."

We look at him. Williams Lake is in the bush; and though many of us have come from the bush, it seems far away here on the edge of the British Properties.

"So you've had experience," Jack says.

"I have! Yeah!" Andy starts laughing, his face red. "There was this one woman I'm telling you she must have weighed over two hundred pounds. She was in the back of this beer parlour in an alley just lying there on a mattress. Guys were just taking turns. It was kind of disgusting."

That summer my dad again loses his job.

He starts to read the want ads. One afternoon when the two of us are sitting in the kitchen, he leans forward and puts his hands around his cup of coffee. "The way things are going, your mother and I might have to buy a mobile home."

I look at him. With his turtle-like neck sticking out of a new, white, fluffy, expensive sweater, he looks old. I grin uneasily. "You're not gonna have to buy a mobile *home*...."

My dad stares at me. "What do you know about it? You don't know anything. Jesus." He shakes his head once and gets up and leaves the room.

Job applications are sent out in the mail.

And then a phone call from Texas. And now everything's happening at once.

A few weeks before we leave, I go walking up into the Properties with Pamela. We hold hands. A shift has occurred: the fact of my leaving has awoken Pamela's feelings for me. "When I heard you were moving," she says, "I went into the closet and stood there in the dark."

My last day in class, the art class girls give me a big sheet of paper on which they've put their handprints in poster paint. And in the late afternoon, as I empty my locker, a trio of black paper cutouts detaches itself from the crowded, sunlit dazzle at the end of the hall. The hall smells of wax; I can hear shouts. The black paper cutouts turn into Alistair and Andy and Ned. I see that Alistair's wearing his corderuey jacket zipped up to his throat.

He looks into my locker. "God, what is all this crap."

"Amazing, isn't it."

"Unbelievable."

He helps me, piling the stuff onto my held-out arms.

Then the locker's cleaned out.

"I guess that's it," I say.

"I guess so," Alistair says.

We stand there awkwardly. "We'll miss you," Ned finally says.

At home I roll the big sheet up; I pack it away, along with the goodbyes of my friends. My family drives to the airport and boards a jet to Seattle. In Seattle we transfer. In the clouds over the American midwest, I write a long letter to Pamela, full of nervous exaltation. I don't know then that in Houston a girl with breasts that are little more than buds and a thatch of hair out of which the tips of her ears peek will turn to me one afternoon in a grade 12 English class and say: "But why are you against capital punishment?"

3. Caribou

I

"How old are you?"

"Nineteen."

"How long have you been living in the United States?"

"Four years."

"So you turned eighteen there."

"I did, yes."

"And did you register for the draft?"

"No."

"You know I could turn you over to the Americans?"

I shook my head.

"Well, I could. And they could call up the FBI, who'd be here in a minute."

I nodded.

The customs official looked at me; then he looked down at something. "I'm trying to figure out what winter boots to buy. I've narrowed the choice down to these two. What do you think?"

He held an Eaton's catalogue out to me, pointed to the two

varieties of boots. Then his finger settled on one. "These are more expensive. But I guess they're better made."

I nodded.

"And I suppose if I can afford good boots I should get good boots. What do you think?"

I grinned. "I guess so."

"So where were you born?"

"St. Boniface, Manitoba."

"I know the place. I lived in Winnipeg for a few years. Bloody cold there sometimes."

"I don't remember it. But I think my parents would agree with you."

He nodded; then waved his hand. "Okay. Welcome back. Enjoy your visit."

I looked at him.

He waved his hand again. "You can go now."

"Okay. Thanks."

I had returned home. I tried to drive carefully. The roads going through the Fraser Valley were narrower than I was used to—black asphalt lined with gravelly ditches. In front of me I saw a sky that seemed infinitely complicated, white and dove-grey, the light constantly shifting so that it seemed to come from everywhere at once. The road signs were tiny. I drove more slowly than I might have on the narrow roads, watching the signs, trying not to make any mistakes.

Then Granville; the Granville Street bridge; and downtown. I parked, looking around—how low all the buildings were—and went into the Hudsons Bay to buy a razor.

So quiet. In that big department store with its old-fashioned wooden floors I saw less than a dozen people. People spoke in cool, self-contained voices. As if they were whispering. And almost no one spoke. I felt something like dismay. Nothing was going on here.

The mood passed. Back outside on Georgia a wind was blowing the clouds across the sky; and though I stood in the middle of downtown I could feel fresh air on my face and I could smell the sea.

Later that afternoon I walked into the Kitsilano Cafe. Three people whom I couldn't quite recognize, as if they were wearing disguises, waved to me from a booth at the back. A beautiful girl in a long suede coat sitting between two hippies.

"Hi Bruce," the girl said; and, as if in a camera lens when the wheel is turned to bring the image into focus, the faces turned into the faces of my friends

Pamela's hair hung straight across her eyebrows and her eyes had a different look. Don's hair surrounded his face like a brown cloud. But Alistair had changed most. He had always dressed quietly; now, wearing an Indian sweater that was too small for him and with his hair hanging to the middle of his back, he looked tramplike. Something inward and dark had entered his demeanor. I still recognized my highschool friends in Don and Pamela; but Alistair had become someone new.

Pamela smiled quickly at me. "I'd say let's drink a coffee and talk. But I need to get cigarettes. There's a store just up the street."

We stepped out into a sprinkle of rain. The air seemed perfumed. I noticed the wooden houses, the red and green and blue asphalt tiles of the roofs. A flock of pigeons flew up in front of us, their wings snapping.

"We're herding birds," I said.

"Here's the store,"

Pamela pushed a tin bar that had the words Orange Crush stamped on it and the light wooden door opened. Wooden walls, a dark wooden floor. Racks of unfamiliar newspapers in English and Chinese. Boxes of oranges and apples. The Chinese proprietor worked quietly unpacking them, his eyes calm in his speck-led face. Behind the counter were rows of Canadian cigarettes and larger packs of tobacco. Vogue, Sportsman, Export A. Looking at them I felt I'd entered a richer world than the one I'd left.

Back on the street Pamela said: "Should we get a coffee? Or what?"

"Let's go to the Egmont," Alistair said.

"I can't. I've got a band practice," Don said. "Besides I've taken a vow. No liquor, alcohol or sex."

"You're in a band?" I said.

"He is," Pamela said. "And he's not kidding about the no drinking or sex. I bite my tongue at you," she added, turning to Don; then said, "Come on, here comes the bus. Or are we gonna go in Bruce's car?"

Walking in the rain up Cordova. On the other side of the hotel, in the harbour trainyards, boxcars shunted, thunder passing from car to car. We could hear tugboats, a mournful sound suggestive to me of the bush that seemed to be just at our backs. Alistair said, "Okay, here we go," and pushed open the scarred black door on which the words "Ladies and Gents" had been painted by hand in white paint.

Vancouver, 1970. A woman with a scarred face, her big breasts bulging behind a dirty tee shirt, grinned at me and stuck her thumb in her mouth and slowly pulled it out. We walked past a stink of piss that wafted out of the men's washroom and sat down at a table near the bar. Then we heard a shout: "Alistair. Over here man!"

We turned. In the cold light coming from the north-facing window sat two hippies: the boy thin, dark-eyed, snub-nosed, with black hair longer even than Alistair's; the girl pretty and pale-eyed, her forehead still stippled with acne. The table at which they sat glittered with glasses of beer.

Alistair said, "Come on, let's go sit with Ray and Jeannine."

As we approached, Ray grinned, heaved himself up and handed Alistair a beer. "Hair of the dog, man." He turned to Pamela and me, smiling so that his eyes were almost shut, and held up his hand in the hippie handshake. "What you doing with this fucker."

"They're old friends," Alistair said. "They're gonna drink with us." Still standing, he raised his head toward the ceiling and downed his beer in one swallow. "Thank you god."

"Praise Jesus," Ray said.

We all sat, and Alistair explained that I had just got back into Van.

"Hey man, great," Ray said. "Where were you?"

"Texas."

"Far out. My dad was in Texas once."

"Where?"

"It was near a place called Alpine. He was working on a ranch. He told a guy it was so flat around there the sun came up out of the earth."

Jeannine said, "Did you come here by yourself?"

I nodded. "But my girlfriend's coming up."

Pamela pushed my shoulder. "You didn't tell us about this! Are you gonna be living with her?"

"I hope so."

Ray said, "Well, if me and Jeannine can do it, so can anyone." He gulped down his beer and reached for another. "Hey Alistair, I saw your new Mrs Nemo story."

"What's this?" I said.

Alistair said, "Oh, I'm trying to write an underground comic."

"Alistair's sort of a genius," Pamela said.

"That's fucking ridiculous," Alistair said.

Two nights later Cate stepped off a plane at the Vancouver Airport and walked quickly toward me, her hair bouncing. We took a room at the Olympia Hotel in North Vancouver. In bed she placed a small towel beneath her buttocks so we wouldn't stain the mattress. The first two days we stayed in bed till noon, whispering to each other about all the things we were going to do in the years ahead.

On the fourth day we moved into a basement apartment at Commercial and Charles that had a wringer-washer on the concrete floor outside our rooms and two wash tubs beside it. And eight months later our life together came undone.

How it ends. With jealousy, tears and a smashed-in bathroom door.

I see her on the Broadway bus. She looks at me as I walk down the aisle, hoping I'll speak to her, sit down with her. I walk past, glaring.

"What's wrong."

"Nothing's wrong."

"Then why won't you talk to me?"

I lie with my back turned to her, staring into a darkness like nothing I've known before.

"So you're moving out."

"Yes."

"Okay."

"Is that all you're gonna say? Haven't you got anything to say to me?" Her cheeks are red, scarred by her tears.

"There's nothing to say."

On a warm bright morning in the spring of 1971 I walked up to the old house on Adanac Street where Alistair lived with Ray and

Jeannine and Moose and Lillian. The house was set on a low hill. I walked slowly up the concrete steps that led to the porch. I had my backpack on my back and carried two enormous suitcases I'd bought in the Salvation Army for a dollar each.

Ray was sitting on the porch, chipping with a hunting knife at its flaking red paint. He squinted at me in the sun.

"Where's the rest of your stuff? You know you can park out front eh?"

"This is all my stuff. I sold my car. It wasn't working."

"What'd you get for it?"

"A hundred bucks."

"Not bad. And it wasn't working."

"No. Neither am I."

"Come on." We passed through the kitchen and Ray opened a door that led to a ladder-like stairway descending into a gloom that smelled of basement. "Down the steps here. Watch your head. I thought you had that job making speaker cabinets."

"Yeah. After Cate left I just didn't want to do it."

"I can dig it. So what you gonna do for money?"

We advanced into the gloom past a ten-speed bike, burlap sacks of potatoes and onions.

"Well. I thought maybe you guys could show me how to get welfare."

"Sure. We can do that. So—here's your room. It's kind of dark, but Jerry—anyway, the guy before you he fixed it up."

"It's terrific."

A bunk bed, a table beneath the bed. Two rows of plank shelving. An old Indian carpet on the concrete floor. A shelf below the window with plants on it. And the window itself, which looked out on a green world, the world of the overgrown bushes and grass behind the house.

While I was looking around, Alistair came in, stooping slightly through the low door that opened onto the backyard.

"You're here."

"Yeah."

"This calls for a joint."

"Right on," Ray said.

We smoked up. Then Alistair said, "Come on, I'll show you my room."

Up the basement steps, already homelike, through the big kitchen, down the hall then up a set of dark old stairs whose wooden boards were in places scuffed raw.

Darkness in the upper hall. But in Alistair's room cool northern light illuminated a swamp. Alistair had always been neat. Now on the floor lay jeans, underwear, the Indian sweater, comic books, *Penthouse* magazines, tensor lamps and cords, ashtrays, a record player, a mattress with a sheet half off it, a couple of filthy-looking pillows, and in one corner a stool and a drafting table with a big lamp next to the table on a tall barrel. Wooden shelves along one wall were filled with more comic books and rapidograph and nib pens and jars of ink.

Ray said, "Show him the comic."

"Sure."

Alistair took down from the top shelf a big binder filled with oversized pages on which rectangles had been drawn.

I flipped through the pages. In each rectangle lived a face, a person, a scene. Registering my friend's achievement, a shock of jealousy swept through me like nothing I'd known before. Alistair had grown beyond me.

"It's a comic book, right. Called *Mrs Nemo*. She's a welfare mom. She's got five kids. She lives on Graveley Street, just up from here. Anyway, the book is about her life. The things that happen to her. Getting welfare, shopping for clothes, having a guy over. All this is ripped off from Ray."

Ray was sitting on the floor, knees up, back against the wall.

"That's right. I'm Alistair's secret weapon."

"What d'you mean?"

Alistair looked at Ray. "Can I tell him?"

"Sure."

"Well, Ray's from a welfare family, and he tells me stories about growing up. His mom—"

"My aunt."

"Sorry. Your aunt. Anyway, he tells me all about it. So I use that."

Ray said, "Yeah, but there's this extra thing."

Alistair said, "Yeah. You ever hear of that cartoon strip *Little Nemo in Slumberland*?"

"No."

"Well, it was one of the first strips. Anyway, in it Little Nemo falls asleep and has these dreams. Well in my story Mrs Nemo doesn't fall asleep. But it's kind of the same. She sits on the couch and lights up a joint, right, or she's cooking, or in one scene she's fucking—and then she has these fantasies. So it gives the story this other dimension. You've got reality and you got poetry."

"Kinda like with R. Crumb." Ray smiled.

Alistair looked at him and laughed. "Yeah."

"What?" I said.

Ray said, "He says his stuff looks like Crumb's."

"Well it does," Alistair said.

"Man, it doesn't," Ray said.

I looked at the inky characters. Mrs Nemo with her nose, her kids. Still feeling the shock brought on by Alistair's achievement, I said, "I don't think it does either. The characters are funny all right, but they look real."

Alistair looked at his book over my shoulder. "Yeah, they're based on real people. I take photographs, right, then I copy them. And I exaggerate things. It's something Crumb does. But I didn't learn it from him. Ned showed me. Remember he used to draw all the time?"

I nodded.

"Yeah. Well, one day I saw a picture he did. He copied one of my shots. And the picture was fantastic. So that gave me the idea. Now I take pictures all the time of things I might use. You know, lamp posts. Street signs. Like that."

Alistair's north-facing window was propped open with a stick. A sudden breeze blew in, bringing the scent of the ocean. Incongruous lace curtains billowed in the wind.

I thought: his mom gave him the curtains. Then I thought: he's my friend. Glancing at him, trying to deal with the shock that had suddenly sickened me, I had a sense of myself as having changed. The grief of Cate's leaving brushed me.

There was a silence. All three of us watched the curtains fly straight out then get sucked back through the open window. It had started to rain.

"Old Ned," I said after a while.

"Yeah."

"Are you in touch with him?"

"No. Not really. He's in Prince George. He works for BC Hydro. He's doing good. Remember how we used to always worry about Ned? Thinking he was under his dad's thumb?" Alistair shook his head. "Uh uh. He's made a life for himself. He's married. He's got a daughter."

"Jesus, he's grown up."

"Yeah."

II

Ray and Jeannine's bedroom always reminded me of a cave. Jeannine's dresses and strings of pearls hung from the slightly open door; her fur coat thrown over a chair looked like a buffalo skin. Little lamps and candles stood everywhere. Thirty or more pictures were tacked to the walls, some cut from magazines, some of them photographs taken by Jeannine. A large yellow piece of lace sat on the chest of drawers, along with small coloured bottles, implements for smoking hashish, a painted ashtray, a teapot, two little bulldogs made of painted plaster. A smell of marijuana and incense gave the room a sexual warmth.

This day Ray sits on the wide bed with his knees up, laughing. Jeannine sits at an angle to him, looking at him and shaking her head.

"*Course* I don't wear gonch," Ray says. "Do you?"

"I'm ashamed to admit that I do."

"No need to be ashamed," Jeannine says. "It just means you come from a better line of upbringing."

"Ha! I don't wash my jeans either. I just stand em up at night and jump into em in the morning."

"Yeah and they stink!" Jeannine pushes at him. Ray falls over; his head lands in Jeannine's lap. "Aw. C'mon. You know they smell sexy."

In the morning I woke to a dark green light. After a few minutes communing with my grief I went up the ladderlike stairs to the kitchen. Moose sat at the table smoking and drinking black coffee. Lillian, her curly hair spilling over her forehead, her eyes calm and intent, stood at the stove.

"Bon matin, monsieur. Porridge for you?"

"Yes please."

She handed me a big bowl, the porridge nutty tasting, heaped with raisins and with two spoonfuls of brown sugar on top.

Ray and Jeannine walked in. Dressed only in his jeans, his black hair hanging to his waist, Ray hugged visible ribs. Jeannine looked around sleepy-eyed and I felt a pang of memory.

After breakfast Ray said: "Anyone wanna smoke up?"

We went into the living rom and sat around the low wooden table. Ray took out a tinfoil-wrapped piece of hashish and filled the bowl of his little pipe. He lit it, held it to his mouth, inhaled sharply, gave a small burping cough.

"Good shit," he said in a strangled voice.

He passed the pipe to me. The harsh smoke rasped my throat.

It had been dull; now the sun broke through the clouds and lit up the stained-glass upper windows of the living room, the colour gone in spots so that the light poured in both prismatic and pure.

Alistair came into the room carrying his coffee, unshaven, his long hair tied back. He put the coffee down and sat on the floor tailor fashion and watched us. After a while he picked up the camera on the table and started taking pictures. We smoked cigarettes and stared at the sunlight, not posing for him.

His coffee finished, he went back upstairs to draw.

"I think I'll start with a tomato juice. Build up to it."

"Good idea."

"Not me," Ray said. He looked around the Niagara Hotel

beer parlour, his face a grinning red mask in the light coming through the red curtains. "Hey there's old Jack and Robert."

"You know them?"

"Yeah. They were friends of my dad. They're a couple old cowboys. Cmon, let's go say hi."

Alistair said, "I've photographed them a few times. Neat guys."

We walked over, each step new to me, something not done before. I thought: Alistair feels it too.

We approached the table. "How you doing, you fuckers," Ray said, and held his hand up. One of the two men, a Native, dark-skinned and black-eyed, shook it gravely. Then the older-looking white man made a fist and touched Ray's hand lightly with it.

The talk turned to horses and ranches. After a while Ray said, "Tell me about my dad."

"You always want to hear about your dad," Robert, the Native man, said.

"So what. Tell me."

"What d'you wanna hear."

"Anything."

"That gives us a lotta latitude," Jack, the white man, said.

"Anything."

Robert made a little motion with his hand to Jack.

"My turn eh. Okay. Well, let me see." Jack sipped his beer, stroked the side of his long red nose. "Let me think. Well, I remember one thing. I was the youngest of the bunch, okay. Robert here was the oldest. But Henry was our leader. He was the cowboss. A little guy. Nice little guy. His knowledge of cattle and horses was unreal. Anyways, him and your dad, they were a lot alike."

He sipped his beer. "Both of them were smart. They were always joking. Funny things. Anyway I remember one time Mel was drawing Robert." He turned to his friend. "You remember that?"

"Here we go."

"My dad was drawing?" Ray said.

"Yeah. Mel used to draw." Jack turned to Robert, who was shaking his head. "Remember, you were sittin against a barn. Sittin on this little stool. Teeny stool. Anyway, you were sittin like this. You had your legs apart and one hand on your hip there. Just like this. Looked like a real tough guy sittin on the throne havin a dump. Anyway Henry comes by and he says: 'You drawing that truculent prick?' And Mel says, 'Uh huh.' And you say—remember this?—you say, 'My what prick?' Henry looks at you. 'Your truculent prick.' Well you looks down. 'My prick don't look like a truck.' 'Look at it again,' Henry says. So you do."

"Ha. Ha."

"After that for months it was, 'Here comes the truculent prick.'"

A hot summer night in the Egmont, the bar packed. On the jukebox Van Morrison's "Wild Night" has been turned up against the roar of the crowd so that it teeters on the edge of distortion:

> *And the wind catches your feet*
> *and sends them flying*

Lillian jumped up, sinuous and bright-eyed. "Come on, somebody dance with me."

Moose said, "Dance with her, Ray."

I don't dance."

Alistair said, "I'll dance with you any time, Lillian."

After they'd gone onto the dance floor, I looked at Ray: "You don't dance?"

"Nope. The way I was brought up. Neither does Moose."

"All right."

I vowed never to dance again.

In the whirl of noise and joy a girl in a tight yellow sweater walked by, fuzzy outline of extravagant tits. Ray looked at me.

"C'mon, let's go into the girl's can."

"Sure."

Staggering among the tables, grins pulling our faces, we walked past the bar to the women's washroom. We sat on the floor just inside, our backs against the tiled wall, staring up at legs rising smooth-thighed to cut-off jeans.

"Hey Mary show me your heart," Ray called out.

Mary unzipped and thumbed her jeans and panties down and bent over, flashing white buttocks on one of which a heart pierced with an arrow had been tattooed.

We stepped out of the women's washroom into a roar. Every table was filled to the edge with glasses of beer. Jeannine was shaking her head in amused dismay. She shouted, "The drinks are on the house."

"Great."

"Yeah. Jack and Robert just came in with a friend of theirs." She leaned toward us and shouted in our ear. "This guy Alex. He's just down from the bush. He laid down three hundred-dollar bills and that's it."

"It's potlatch time!" Lillian shouted.

"How much money we got."

"About forty bucks."

"Okay. Let's put it in the pot."

"I got a twenty."

"I got a few bucks."

"We'll drink the house down!"

Ray leaned across the table. "Hey Moose. Too bad you don't work in the bush any more." He grinned at me. "He used to come in here, spend five hundred bucks a night."

"Moose is an Indian *chief*," Lillian said.

"Is that right, Moose?"

"You're damn right."

"And he drinks like a chief."

'You too, Lillian."

"I can drink."

An hour later the mood had changed. Ray was leaning forward, questioning Alex.

"You knew my mom?"

"Yeah." Alex had been drinking steadily.

"What was she like? What did she look like?"

He gestured with his chin. "He can tell you."

Jack leaned forward. He stroked his nose. "She was a very good looking gal. Hair to her waist and she wore those short shorts. She had a very fine rump on her. Nice hips. Beautiful girl."

Robert said, "She was the first girl I ever saw roping. I remember she went up to the Williams Lake Stampede with Mel one time and she tried to get into that mountain race. She could ride like the dickens."

Looking at Alex, Ray said, "How old was my mom when you knew her?"

"What?"

"My mom. How old was she?"

Alex stared at him, his eyes sodden. After a minute he said, "Fifteen. I don't know."

"And they fell in love, her and my dad?"

Alex's head jerked. "What in the fuck kind of question is that—'and they fell in love.'"

Jack stared at him. "Alex, this is Mel's boy you're talking to. Of course they fell in love. You know that."

"I don't know that. He was her meal ticket, that's what I know. She thought he was white. And that was it. She wanted to go out with a white man. She didn't want any fucking Indian. That was all it was. That's why she wore those shorts. That's why she pranced around like that. I don't think she loved him. Mel was weak."

Jeannine stood up and touched Ray's arm. "Come on Ray, let's go."

"No. What do you mean, weak?"

"I mean he was always playing. He played at being a cowboy. He'd wear those batwing chaps and that old hat and he'd sit on his horse like he was the lone ranger. With that stupid grin."

My cheeks had flushed. I said, "Why are you talking about Ray's dad like that?"

"When did this become your fucking business?" He stared at me. Then he turned to Ray. "I'll tell you what. Your dad could work. You know what work is?"

"Yeah I know what work is."

He nodded once. "Yeah. To get those cattle to Clinton and then down to Perry Ranch, it was about a hundred miles."

He kept looking at Ray. "Why do you want to know all this about him?"

"Because he's my dad. What do you think."

Alex kept looking at him. "That doesn't tell me why you want to know about him and Elsie."

"Well I guess that's none of your business."

"You smartmouthing me?"

"What do you think?" Ray said.

"I think you are."

"Well that's too fucking bad."

Alex stood up from his chair and leaned over and clubbed Ray in the mouth with his fist. Moose grabbed him. "Okay, that's it, you."

"Fuck you."

Robert grabbed one of Alex's arms and jerked it hard up

behind Alex's back. Alex shouted. His eyes watered and snot poured from his nose.

Richard and a heavyset man from behind the bar came over. Moose said, "Get him out of here. Or I'll kill him."

Alex was vomiting. Robert still had his arm jerked up behind his back.

The summer ended. Days of grief, drunken nights immersed in happiness. Electric green leaves shone in the streetlight outside the Egmont's windows, a vivid sight. With my black toque pulled down to my eyebrows, I felt at home in this crowd of friends.

One night Ray said, "Hey Bruce, you got company."

"What d'you mean?"

"Look."

I looked where he pointed. Cate stood in the doorway. My heart jumped in my chest at the shock. She walked toward me, wearing a short black jacket and tight white jeans. Her hair, more sophisticated now, darkened her eyes. Cate's presence in this room where I sat with reprobates and worse made me feel I was living in a ballad in which men might ride into town on unshod horses.

"Can I sit?"

"I'll get you a chair."

"That's okay. I'll sit on your lap."

"She sat and put her arm around me. I noticed the lipstick on her lips, the mascara that made her eyes brilliant. I could feel my erection press against my jeans.

"So are you gonna buy me a beer?"

"Here. Have mine."

She drank, then handed the glass to me. "You look good."

"So do you."

"Are you gonna introduce me to your friends?"

"Why not?"

Later that night she whispered in my ear, "Let's go to my place. We'll get a cab."

"Okay."

Urgent, dazed with it, we walked with our arms around each other up the stairs to her little room. Satin bedspread and soft lights. Holding each other, our bodies pressed together, we fell onto her bed. While she took off her clothes I kissed her mouth and moved my hands on her. Then her glowing face and naked body were beneath me.

"God I love you."

"I love you too."

A casket of happiness spilled open inside me.

That was the last time. At the end of September she moved to San Diego for good.

Hours of endless rocking through the long afternoons.

One evening I stepped out onto the back porch, too sad to do anything, too restless to sit still.

"Hey Bruce."

"Hey Moose. How you doing."

"C'mere. Have a cigarette," he said. "I'm watching the evening come on."

I leaned against the railing of the back porch and took the cigarette Moose offered.

"I was just looking at that chain saw down there," he said, "and thinking I've never seen one that wasn't temperamental. It takes nothing to flood em."

I nodded.

"You ever use one of those old two-man Johnson saws? It took two men to lift one. Thank Christ they're safer now. They cut off when you're not running them. Used to be they'd keep running and it was nothing to accidentally rip yourself up. I've seen a man go right through his foot, cut it in two, that way." He paused, looking down at the saw. "I remember fixing those things. Big goddamn saws. Hit a stone or a knot and whap that thing just made you lose your balance and there you go."

He flicked his cigarette down onto the grass. "Look at those mountains. I love watching the light move up them like that."

I looked with him at the North Shore drowning in shadow.

"Moose, how come you're in such a good mood?" I asked. "Clean pants, clean white shirt. What is this?"

"Been pearl diving all day."

"What's that?"

"You never heard of that?" He stared at me. "I was washing dishes. Down at the Fraser Arms."

"That's good."

"Yeah. Lillian's coming back home too."

"You talked to her?" I felt relief. The house had been somber with her missing.

"Yeah. And she's working again. That's how I got the job."

I stood in the doorway looking into the kitchen at my friends sitting around the table. A warm scene in the wintertime; but I felt uncertain of my place among them.

"Come on and drink with us Bruce."

We're gonna get hammered on Five Star."

"Alistair here is gonna make us famous. He's gonna sell *Mrs Nemo* and we'll all have money."

"That's right."

I sat next to Alistair, who was bent over a sheet of paper working with a piece of charcoal. "What're you drawing?"

"Ray's dad."

"Huh." I sipped the whiskey Moose had given me.

"Jack and Robert described him for me. But I can't get the eyes right."

The thought came to me. "Give him Ray's eyes."

Alistair looked at me. He looked at his work. "Right. Of course. Fucking A."

He looked at the group seated around the table drinking. "Look, I'm just gonna go upstairs and finish this off."

Some minutes later he came back down the stairs and showed the drawing to Jack and Robert. They leaned forward, staring at it. Robert's dark eyes were reflective. Jack finished his whiskey and wiped his mouth. He looked at his friend. "What do you think?"

"That's him."

Jack said, "Ray, that's your dad. That's him."

Ray stared at the drawing for a long moment. "He looks good."

"He was a good-looking guy," Jack said.

"He was," Robert said. "You know, seein that, I just remembered something." He drank his whiskey. "You might like this, Ray. It was when I met your dad. It was just about a little after I got my first job up at Basque ranch. We were diggin irrigation ditches and that was hard work. For a little Indian boy like me that was bloody hard. Those irrigation ditches were twenty-four inches apart. Dug with pick and shovel. But I got some money. And the first thing I did, I bought a cowboy hat.

"I remember Mel said, 'You gotta have a hat.' So I bought one. Got it up in Clinton. Nice hat too. Cost me thirty-seven dollars. Anyway, I put it on. Mel walks all around me, stroking his chin. Then he says: 'It's too new. You look like a dude. Give me that hat.' So I give it to him. Then he says: 'Wait here a sec.' 'Okay.' So I wait. He comes back, he's got a shovel. He starts diggin a hole in the ground. 'Whatcha doin?' He says: 'Just wait.' He digs the hole and then he puts the hat in the hole. 'What in the hell you doin?' 'Just wait,' he says. He puts the hat in the hole, then he starts puttin dirt in. Fills up the hole. I'm thinking: Hold on here. Then he digs up the hat. Steps on it. He walks on it eh? Back and forth. Then he picks it up and he dusts if off and he hands it to me. Says, 'I don't want you to look like a dude.'"

He smiled at Ray and Ray smiled back. "You were friends."

"We were. It didn't matter to him one bit that I was an Indian boy. I knew almost from the first day I met him that we'd be friends. And I needed a friend. I was pretty alone."

"Huh."

Ray looked at the drawing. After a minute he turned to Alistair, tapped a fist on his shoulder. "Thanks man."

The third bottle was empty. Moose lit the kitchen stove against the cold; after a while Jeannine, sweating, opened the door to the back porch. We piled outside, past the cases of beer bottles.

Careful as a cat, Alistair stepped down the back steps. We followed him and watched him weave out into the yard. It was bitterly cold, the full moon shining. Frost had whitened the grass. Alistair lay on his back on the frozen ground and crossed his legs as if he was sitting on a chair. Sick sweat shone on his forehead and cheeks. "Ladies and gentlemen," he muttered, "I'm temporarily indisposed."

Shivering in the cold, Ray grinned down at him; then he knelt and kissed Alistair on the lips. I felt loneliness rise in me like a tide.

The girl sat on the couch across from me, her eyes nearly shut. Her skirt had ridden halfway up her thighs. Ray and Jeannine had left.

"Come on, sit with me," she said.

I crossed the room and sat beside her. She kissed me, her lips soft and wet. I placed my hand on her thigh. I moved the skirt up, more and more excited; then I came in my pants.

"What's wrong?" she said, splayed back on the couch, her

legs apart. "Why are you stopping?"

"I don't know."

I pulled her skirt down, smelling the semen at the front of my pants.

A week later, no longer able to bear either myself or others, I moved out of the house.

On the Egmont jukebox Joan Baez was singing "The Night They Drove Old Dixie Down." The voices and laughter faded. I listened to the exalted music and imagined Cate walking in the door. The hallucination took on fantastic clarity. She was stepping through the doorway. She was walking among the tables, her hair in her eyes. She was walking over to me. She sat down. She smiled and leaned forward and held out her hands.

III

"Have you ever worked in the bush before?"

"Yeah, I have."

"Do you have any camping gear?"

"What do you mean by camping gear?"

"A sleeping bag."

"Sure."

What about work clothes."

"What kind?"

"Well, have you got work boots, rain gear, that kind of thing."

"Yeah, I've got that."

"Good logging boots?"

"Absolutely."

"Okay. You've got the job."

Overheated in the two wool shirts and thick sweater I'd worn to bulk myself up, I stepped out into weak sunlight. Just up the street a large sign advertised Pierre Paris & Sons. I went in and bought the heaviest pair of logging boots I could find.

The plane droned and droned through the air above Vancouver Island. Finally it landed at an airport in Port Hardy that looked like a rural soccer field—a strip of dirt cut out of the bush and lined with creosoted twelve by twelves.

Hal and Barry and I climbed out of the plane. Three men in yellow rain slickers walked toward us.

The smallest of the three smiled. "Okay. I hope you guys are ready to work. I'm Andy Dupre. You're gonna hate me because every morning I'm gonna wake you up eh. Boy, I'm gonna crack the whip. This is George Little and Jerry Lafontaine. Hal, you're gonna partner with me. Barry, you go with George. Bruce, you go with Jerry."

Jerry and I looked at each other. I saw a grey face, nervous eyes, thick lips whose edges seemed to have been shaped with a knife. He walked over and touched the Pierre Paris and Sons boots that were tied to the back of my pack.

"Those your boots?"

"Yeah, they're my boots."

"They're no good. Come on. We'll go to the store. Got some time before the chopper. Buy you some good boots."

"I don't have any money."

"I'll buy em. You can't work in those."

In the gloom of Port Hardy's general store, Jerry said, "You smoke?"

I nodded.

"Get a couple tins of tobacco. What kind?"

I saw him reach toward the Sportsman tins beside the Players and Export.

"I'll get two Sportsman."

"Good. Now here. This is the kind of boot you need."

He held out a pair of rubber boots that laced up. Their soles were studded with screwed-in metal spikes.

"These'll do you. Those are no good."

"Okay."

"What size you take."

"Nine."

He looked at the boxes. "Ask the guy if they've got any size nine."

I did. The shopkeeper shook his head.

"Okay, we'll take a ten." He picked out a pair of boots and

handed them to me.

I held them up and sniffed inside them. "They've got that nice new rubber boot smell."

"Yah, well, try them on."

I did.

"They're too big."

"That's okay. You put a piece of foam in em. You'll be all right."

We went back to the landing strip and waited. After a while the helicopter came down out of the rain, its rotors maintaining a deep whoop whoop whoop.

"Come on," Andy said. "And keep your head down!" We ran toward the open side door.

Inside we sat on the floor of the helicopter. George, a Native man in a black cowboy hat, sat on his pack with his back against the wall across from me, his hands clasped on his thigh in a pose that made him look dignified and calm. I copied him.

Twenty minutes later the helicopter descended through the trees to a landing pad made of crisscrossed logs. We stepped out into darkness and sublimity. We were in the temperate rain forest, a cold jungle with rain falling, twenty feet from the edge of a canyon that dropped and dropped to a creek like a thin string. All around us in the rainy blear was a no-man's-land of mud in which lay logs, metal poles, stakes, gas cans, oil drums and chainsaws, strewn about like the equipment of war. Huge trees rose into mist, their tops invisible; up under the trees stood a beleagured outpost of canvas tents.

"Well, isn't this pretty," Hal said.

"Let go of your cocks and grab your socks! It's daylight in the swamp!"

"Uh."

Come on. Get up. Get up!"

"It's raining."

"It's not raining. Get up."

Hal and Barry and I, the camp's youngest members, sat on the edges of our cots. Silently we pulled on our clothes. Damp socks, filthy jeans, filthy shirts, mud and sweat stiffening them as if with a kind of crust. Then our boots and rain gear. Still not speaking we walked in the drizzle to the cook tent.

A string of electric lights lit our way. Mud underfoot. The generator roared. In the tent we smelled coffee, cigarettes, pancakes, fried ham.

Serious business here; grim men. We sat on the bench squeezed in between Andy and Jerry and George, who barely moved to make room for us.

There was little talk. All thought of Vancouver and what I'd left behind there was gone. At this moment, eating eggs and ham and pancakes, I knew only the pain of getting started.

After breakfast the three of us walked back to our tent and got our packs together.

Barry said, "Where d'you keep your tape?"

"In my shirt pocket."

"Good idea."

"Yeah you can get it when you need it. I always got a roll in there. And in my pack."

"Fucking unfair the guys don't carry anything," Hal said.

"They carry a compass," Barry said.

"Yeah. Big fucking deal."

"Those fucking chain saws get heavy."

"My pack stinks of fucking oil."

"Fucking trapper nelsons. They're heavy as a son of a bitch."

Andy stuck his head in the door. Grim, intent, he said: "Come on you boys, let's go. Let's go."

"We're coming."

Into the grey morning. After half an hour Jerry and I left the main trail and headed into the bush, starting our line. While we were battling through a thicket of willows up a steep hill, the sun came out. Sweat poured from me. The pack on my back, heavy with a chain saw, stakes and cans of gas and oil, started to swing from side to side. Smells of gasoline and oil were coming from my pack. Cold sweat popped out on my face. My stomach, tight with pancakes and ham, convulsed. My mouth filled with saliva.

"Jerry, hold on a second," I called and dropped to my knees and vomited.

Jerry looked at his compass then walked ahead of me into the bush, paying out the sixty-six-foot-long line. He dropped out of sight. When he came to the end of the line I called, "Chain!" The line went slack. I followed it, cutting at the bushes with my machete, making a hint of a trail. Every few yards I tied a piece of pink flagging tape. When I got to where Jerry was standing, near the bottom of a small gully, I inserted a stake and we marked the spot.

"Okay, now. There's a canyon here. We got to find a log across it."

We had come to a ravine. A creek rushed far below. I walked a hundred yards or so in either direction looking for a fallen log over the ravine.

"I can't find anything."

"Give me the saw."

I gave it to him. He looked at the trees, found one that was close and tall enough and leaning in the right direction, then expertly made two cuts, one on either side of the tree.

"Stand back."

He pushed; with a thunderous crash the tree fell across the ravine, its branches on the far side.

"Okay. Now come on."

He walked lightly across the bare trunk.

I sat on the trunk. Then, foot by foot, pulling myself forward, I inched across on my bum. Jerry watched. He neither shook his head nor nodded, just kept his pale eyes on me.

"I'm sorry I took so long."

"Okay."

I stood on the log.

Jerry called out, "Just look straight ahead. And run."

I balanced the pack. Then I stepped forward, the spikes in my boots digging into the wood, walking quickly, eyes straight ahead, not looking down at the white water rushing ceaselessly past below.

"Chain!"

I stared down at the steep gully. Then I stepped into it, swinging my machete. And slipped, falling three feet into a thicket so dense I hung in midair caught by the branches.

"Where are you?"

"I'm here."

Jerry peered down at me.

"You fall?"

"Yeah."

"Well, you better get up."

"Chain!"

I whapped a willow with my machete. The machete bounced on the hard dark branch and sliced into my thumb to the bone. Dark red plush. Then a deep sting and the blood started to pour.

I called, "Hey Jerry, I cut myself pretty good."

He walked back and looked at my held-out thumb. "Boy. Here." He pulled a faded handkerchief out of his back pocket. "Use this. Wrap it around." He watched me do as he said. "Okay.

We'll go back. Get that fixed up." He nodded. "Yeah. Good thing you cut yourself now, not later."

We trudged back to camp. The cook, who was also the first aid attendant, wrapped a proper bandage around my thumb. He looked at me. "You know, you should go to a hospital and get stitches for this."

"I guess so."

"Are you gonna go?"

"No."

A few days later when I got back from work I found Hal lying face down on his cot.

I said, "You're back early."

"Yeah. I got a stomach ache."

I was taking off my boots when Andy stepped into the tent. He looked at his partner. "Hey you, get out of here."

"What?"

"Get out. Get out. The chopper's waiting. And don't come back."

He turned and left.

"Okay. Let's have a smoke."

We sat on the big rock we had reached and looked at the bush around us.

After a minute Jerry said, "This is good bush. It's been logged. You hear that bird?"

A thin piping.

"Yeah."

"Bush gets too old, no animals, no birds. Nothing. You need to log it. Or you need a fire."

"I see what you mean."

"Nice day for work."

I looked at the wet bush all around us, the oppressive sky.

89

"No sun. Easy on the eyes. Bit of rain. Then you can work."

"Okay."

He watched me eat my sandwich and my bag of nuts and raisins and smarties.

"You like to eat."

"Yeah."

"Good."

He put out his cigarette on his hand then put the butt in his pocket. "Okay, let's go."

We climbed up to the top of the ridge. Jerry turned and looked at me. "There's a road ahead, going our way."

"Good."

Walking on the road's flat surface I felt I was walking six inches above the ground. We passed a rockpit, then saw three trailors. The trailors sat in the shadowless light among rusted coils of cable, old magazines turned yellow by the sun, thrown-out underwear, oil cans, oil drums, car parts, plastic kids' toys, whiskey bottles and beer bottles by the hundreds: camp life.

We walked toward the trailors, our steps loud, the spikes scraping on the gravel.

Then Jerry stopped. "Did you hear something?"

"No."

"It sounded like a kid."

We listened. Something about the trailors in the shadowless light made the hairs stand up on my neck. We stood still in the middle of the road.

"A kid?"

"Somebody shouting."

We listened. Then Jerry said, "Okay, Let's go."

After lunch it rained hard. We crossed gully after gully choked with willows. I'd been wearing a black and white checked shirt; when it caught on a snag that afternoon, it ripped apart like cheese cloth.

Back in camp I limped into our tent with my mudheavy boots still on and walked across the plywood floor, spikes sinking in, and dropped facedown on my cot. I felt too tired to go to the cook tent for supper.

Terry came in, a boy whose dad was a fisherman. He had replaced Hal. He was part Chinese, with a round face, lidded eyes. He fiddled with his transistor; after a minute he looked at me. "Hey, you made a mess. Why don't you clean up after yourself."

"Why don't you fuck off."

All thoughts of Cate had disappeared. In their place was tiredness and fitful exhilaration. Then one day after supper, a week or so before the job was to end, the sun came out.

"It's gonna stay," Andy said. "Sun from here on in."

He waved his arm and I saw it was a beautiful early evening in June. Patches of blue sky overhead. In the steaming moist air, the sun flooded through the trees in nearly straight lines and made in the haze a kind of luminous counterforest.

Andy said, "Come on. Sit with me. Let's have a smoke."

We sat on rounds of log in the warm sun and smoked.

After a minute he said, "How are you getting on with Jerry?"

"Not bad. For the first week or so I was always falling."

"Sure."

"I could tell he was impatient. But he didn't lose his temper. A couple days ago he said to me, 'Boy, at first I thought: he's no good. But you came through. You stuck to it.' So that was okay."

"Good. Good."

I looked at Andy, wanting to say more. I added: "I have to say, I was more impressed by the first part of what he said. I imagine he had to hold back his anger."

I wasn't sure how Andy would take this. To make up for it I said, "Anyway, he sure is good with a chain saw."

"Well, he was a faller. You seen how thick his wrists are eh?"

91

I nodded. "They're wide as his hands."

"That's right. He's damn good. But I don't know about him having to hold back his anger." Andy blew out cigarette smoke. "Now don't spread this around. But Jerry killed a man. This man was sleeping with his wife eh. And Jerry got in a rage and beat him to death. They put him in prison. He was there seventeen years. And in prison all the anger got washed out of him."

Jerry had stopped. When I caught up to him, he said, "You hear that sound?"

"Yeah. It sounds like somebody calling."

We moved through the bush. We could see the light of a clearing ahead. We walked towards it. The bush thinned out; and then we walked across open duff, soft underfoot, to the edge of a high cliff with the world blue and limitless in front of us. Thin strips of cloud moved across the sky and the sea stretched out in the light that seemed to come from every direction but was only the open sun on our faces.

A hundred yards straight below us, in the water in front of the cliff face, dozens of seals barked and screamed at each other, playing, fighting, diving then coming up again. We stared down at them. The open ocean stretched to the horizon. For maybe ten minutes, Jerry and I sat near the cliff's edge and smoked and watched the world.

IV

"So Bruce. What you gonna do with all your money?"

"I don't know."

"What about you, Terry?"

Terry thought about it. "I'm not sure. Go into business with my dad."

"God, you're so fucking serious man. Don't you ever have fun?" Barry looked out the window at the seagulls flying past. "Look at those fucking birds. Can they ever fucking move."

I said, "Barry, you got to stop saying fuck every fucking second word. We're not in the bush anymore."

"Fuck off. We're on the ferry. Might as well be the bush." He grinned. "Fuck I got three thousand bucks for two month's work and I can't believe it!" He leaned forward and plucked at my arm. "Haven't seen that shirt before."

"I kept it at the bottom of my pack."

"Looks good."

Horseshoe Bay.

We watched Terry put his pack in the back seat of his dad's car and then climb into the front.

He stuck his head out the window. "See you guys!"

"You take care man!"

After the car had driven off, Barry shifted his pack and looked at me. "You wanna come for a beer? There's a great bar here."

"No, you go ahead. I'm gonna catch the West Van bus and

then head downtown."

He smiled. "You got a fucking girlfriend, don't you. Okay. You take care now."

"You too."

We shook hippie-style and Barry walked away, his head bobbing, bent under the weight of his pack. After a few yards he half-turned and called out, "Don't forget to fuck her for me!"

On a rainy day in late June I got a room at the Niagara Hotel. Sitting on my bed that afternoon, I put on my new clothes: a pale yellow shirt, button front Levi jeans and a pair of black cowboy boots. I looked at myself in the mirror. Then I took out my bank book and looked at it. Never in my life had I had so much money. I walked around the room and looked out the window at Burrard Inlet. Then I went down to the lobby.

"Is there a phone I could use?"

The man at the counter pointed. "Over there."

My heart slamming in my chest, I dialled Cate's number in San Diego.

Hissing, crackling.

I dropped in quarters. Then, from thousands of miles away, three rings; and then a man's voice: "Hello?"

"Hi. I was wondering if Cate was in."

"No, she's not here now. Can I take a message?"

I had never heard this phrase before. "No, that's okay," I said, and hung up.

The next day I walked up Hastings to the old house. Three people I didn't know were sitting in the living room on the couch, long-haired hippies in leather vests and jeans, one wearing a Daniel Boone fur cap. They sat silently, like people waiting to see the doctor.

I went upstairs. Alistair's door was open and his room was in even more disarray than usual. No one in Lillian's and Moose's. No one in Ray's and Jeannine's.

While I was walking back down the stairs, Ray and Jeannine came in the front door. Ray wore a sweater under his jean jacket, Jeannine had on her fur coat.

"Hey, you're back!" Ray grinned, held up his hand and we shook. Jeannine hugged and kissed me. "So how'd it go?"

"Great. I'm rich. I'll tell you all about it. But who's the guys in the living room? And how come you're all dressed up?"

"They're friends of Alistair's."

"They're from *The Georgia Straight*. They're running a cartoon of his."

I felt the old shock of jealousy. "*Mrs Nemo*?"

"No, a different thing. He started doing it about a month ago."

"Why are they here?"

"We're all going to pick up Alistair. He was in jail. They got him for possession. And apparently he's got gonorrhea."

At the UBC lawcourts, I looked at my friend with dismay. He wore his old Indian sweater that was too small in the sleeves, and he stood in the dock with his head bent forward, greasy hair falling over his face.

Later, barely glancing at Ray and Jeannine and me, he whispered, "Thanks for coming man." His breath stank.

That afternoon Alistair and I went to the Egmont. As usual, we rolled up the sleeves on our shirts and held our glasses of beer with our left hands even when the glasses were on the terrycloth table. But the words died in our throats.

Our friendship had changed the first time I'd looked at his comic book. And slowly, as the winter had turned into spring, that change had come between us.

Now we sat as if separated by a wall. Each of us was living a different life from what he'd had before. We were young, trying hard to be men, and we didn't know a way back to the boys we had been. We drank, but we had nothing to say to each other.

Two weeks later I again walked up Hastings to the house. That morning Caltex had asked if I'd like to go up to Watson Lake to work as a bull cook. I'd said yes. Now I wanted to say goodbye.

It started to rain when I reached Adanac Street. Within seconds it was pouring, the rain bouncing off the street and turning the asphalt white. Moose's car was parked out in front of the house and Ray was sitting in it. When he saw me he opened the door. "Come on, get out of this shit."

I climbed in. "So this your new home?"

"Naw. We're gonna try to find Lillian. She took off again."

I nodded. "How's Moose?"

"He's a little fucked up." Ray looked out the window at the rain.

"What about you?"

"I'm okay."

"You don't sound spectacular."

"Aw…Jeannine and I were fighting over the new guy in your room."

"What, was she…?"

"Nah. No, no, no. It's like, he's selling coke. And she's worried about the cops coming around." Ray sighed. "So that's what it is….Yeah, and damn bloody Lillian's all screwed up. And Moose is fucked up."

"I've never been in his car before."

"It's great eh?"

"It's like a fucking tool shed in here."

"There's comic books too. On the back seat. They're Alistair's."

I turned and looked. On the back seat lay a welding cap, a bunch of welding rods, a jar of pickles and about a dozen comics ranging from *Donald Duck* to *The Fabulous Furry Freak Brothers.*

While we sat there waiting out the downpour and reading old Scrooge McDuck books, Moose came down the steps with his coat over his shoulders. He walked over to the car. I opened the door.

"Push over."

"Okay."

Moose looked unhappy. He sat for a moment in the driver's seat, his hands on the wheel. Then he turned to me. "Want to go for a ride?"

"Where to?"

"To pick up Lillian."

Ray said, "Where is she?"

"I don't know. That's the thing. I think she might be down at Musqueam. Or she might be with a guy named Al."

"Okay."

"I want to find her. I want to bring her back. That's why I'm asking you two eh."

I said, "Sure you want us to come?"

"Uh huh." Moose started rolling a cigarette. He rolled the tobacco in a Zig-Zag cigarette paper held between the thumbs and first two fingers of his hands. He licked the paper. He popped an Eddy match on his thumbnail, lit the cigarette, blew out the smoke.

"I'll tell you why I want you to come. It's just me she won't come back. I know it. Not this time. But with you guys there I think she will."

I said, "Why'd she go this time?"

"Same as always." He looked at me. "She's unhappy. I don't know. Maybe she's bored with me. She wants to party."

"Okay." I looked at Ray and he nodded. "Sure, let's go."

"Good. Let's go then."

The car was cold. Because he drove so rarely, Moose was

cautious. He let out the choke, then when the car started we sat in it for a couple of minutes without moving. Moose turned the heater on and the car filled with the warm winter smell of a car heater. Then we turned down the alley and onto Adanac and then up Clark Drive to Broadway.

The clouds were dark as a drain pipe overhead when we drove into South Vancouver; and by the time we reached the small Chinese cafe by the reserve it was raining hard again. A wind had blown up and the rain ripped across the windshield. In the bush just beyond the small dirt lot the wind was lifting the leaves on the trees and exposing their pale undersides.

"I wish I'd worn a jacket," Ray said.

I nodded. Walking from the car to the door of the old cafe we became soaked.

We walked into the cafe just as a train went by. The ketchup and vinegar bottles, the salt and pepper shakers and the cups in their saucers all shivered a bit.

We sat down on the low swivel stools. Moose said to the counterman, "Have you seen Lillian?"

"Lillian?"

"Lillian Louie. My wife. She's short, like me. She comes here a lot."

The counterman shrugged.

"She's got curly black hair. She was wearing a cowboy shirt, a black cowboy shirt with red flowers on it."

"Oh yeah. She was here. Gone now."

"When was she here?"

"About an hour ago. Yeah, she come in with friends."

'Friends?"

"Two guys."

"Oh boy."

Moose rolled and lit a cigarette and hunched forward. After a minute he said, "Where do you think they went?"

"Who went?"

"My wife, and the two guys you said she was with."

"Ah. Maybe back to the guy's place—maybe some place else." The Chinese man took plates and cups to the sink. "Maybe the reserve," he called out.

We went out to the car. It had stopped raining, but the wind was still blowing and the air was cold. White and grey clouds were moving fast across the sky.

Moose drove out from the muddy lot. He drove out to the highway and along it for a couple of miles, and then drove up a rutted dirt road that led into the bush near where the highway came close to the Fraser River.

About a mile up the road we stopped. A small log cabin stood in a cleared space. There were no cars parked nearby. Moose opened his door; we all got out.

"Maybe you should stay here by the car," Moose said.

He walked over to the cabin door and knocked on it. Then he took the axe that was in a stump by the door and used the back of the axe's head to knock louder. The door was thick pine wood, and even with the axe head the sound was dull. There was no one there. Moose looked in the small window and then disappeared around the back of the cabin.

After a minute he walked toward us. "No one's home."

"So what now," I said.

"I guess we drive back," Moose said. He stood still for a moment, staring into the distance. "Okay then. That's what we'll do. We'll drive back. Check in at the Chink's again."

Driving back the sun came out, raw and brilliant. Lillian's Vauxhall was parked outside the front of the cafe. We went in. She was sitting down at the end by herself, smoking and drinking a coffee. Her curly hair was disordered, but that only made her more pretty. Moose walked toward her. We walked behind him. She looked up and shook her head.

Moose sat down on the stool beside her. Ray and I stayed standing.

"I've come to take you home," Moose said.

"Take me home?"

"Something like that."

"Something like that is more like it," Lillian said.

"I brought Ray and Bruce."

"I see that. Sit down boys. Eh boys," Lillian said. "You want to sit with me? Move over, Moose. Let Bruce and Ray sit."

Moose got up and Lillian moved to his stool. "You boys sit on each side of me eh?"

I sat on her left and Ray sat on her right.

"You boys look good enough to eat with your wet hair." Lillian was flushed. Behind the coffee and cigarettes I could smell alcohol.

"So Moose brought you boys to bring me home. That's sweet. Why would I go otherwise eh Louie? Why, huh? You tell me. Should I go with you?"

"I want you to come with me," Moose said.

"Should I bring Al?"

"No."

"Eh boys? Should I bring Al? Me and Moose and Al?"

"No," Moose said. "Don't bring Al."

"No Lillian," Ray said. "Why don't you just come with us."

"Oh you boys." And then Lillian leaned forward and held my face in her hands and kissed me on the lips. Her lips tasted of alcohol. Her face was big and close and her still-drunken eyes held me for a second then let go. I watched her turn on her stool and kiss Ray.

"Come on then, let's get going," she said.

We got up from our stools and she put her arms out and pulled Ray and me close to her. As we approached the door her hips brushed against us. I could feel the seams of her tight jeans against me. Her small hard hand gripped my shoulder. The three of us went through the door together, barely squeezing through.

"Whew, it's bright," Lillian said. "Hurts my eyes." She pulled away and walked ahead of us. "I'll drive my car," she called back.

Moose watched her helplessly. His eyes were dull. He said nothing. I waited for him to speak. Ray called out, "Come on Lillian. Come with us. Leave your car there. We can get it later."

We all got in Moose's car. Ray and I sat in the back with the comic books.

Lillian said, "Eh Moose, roll me a cigarette."

"Okay."

Moose rolled her a cigarette.

"You're shaking," Lillian said.

"I got wet."

"Yeah, sure."

He finished the cigarette and handed it to her, his hand trembling. He popped a match on his thumbnail and held it out. Lillian lightly held his hand as he lit her cigarette. She blew out a long drifting plume of smoke, then leaned over and kissed him. He sat stiffly, letting her do it.

After a minute his face relaxed. The grief left it. Driving carefully, he turned onto the highway. It started to rain again. Moose turned on the wipers. Once we'd been driving awhile his right hand left the wheel. He placed it on Lillian's shoulder. She reached up and put his hand on her thigh. Looking over the bench seat, I saw how Moose's hand gripped her thigh through her jeans. Going down Broadway Lillian started to sing, a French song I'd last heard in Hinton when I was about eight years old: *Va toujours l'arire.*

V

The cabbie said, "So how d'you like Watson Lake?"

"So far so good. It's sure light out."

"Yep. Ten at night and you can read a book. You like to drink? There's two dozen bars in town."

"Sounds good."

"I bet there's a bar for every ten people." He drove. "Yeah. Every ten people I bet you there's a bar." He looked at me. "You just starting work?"

"Yeah."

"Well, if you haven't got the money you can pay me later."

"Really?"

"Sure. I'll see you around. Everybody knows me. Just ask for Tony the cabbie you need a ride."

I smiled. "I guess I'm not in Vancouver any more. Don't worry, I can pay."

"Good. Good. Good. But if you need a cab you just ask for me. Tony the cabbie." He drove. "That's me. Tony the cabbie. You just gotta ask."

He pulled up to a two-storey motel faced with pink and grey stucco. A half dozen big trucks, their undersides muddy, were lined up in the lot.

"Okay, here's your motel."

My room was on the second floor. I lay on the motel bed and grinned. Then I got up and looked out the window at a line of spruce trees and a strip of luminous sky. I smiled again. Then I went out to have a drink.

In the centre of town I stepped from a hotel lobby into a bar carpeted in swirls of red and black. A Native man coming in behind me, not noticably drunk, was refused entry.

"You can't go in there," the big man at the door said.

"Why not."

"Because I say so, that's why not. Come on, get out."

Later that night, walking down Watson Lake's few streets, I saw two small, round-faced men in parkas who looked as if they'd arrived from off the Tibetan steppes. I couldn't place them. Then I thought: Eskimos. A bit later I saw more. Drunks, Native and white, wandered the streets.

Walking back to the motel I noticed the luminous light. It spread over the dusty streets like the light at a night-time baseball game. It produced a sense of wakefulness, a kind of steady excitement. I walked up the motel steps to my room and and lay on my bed and ate a bag of potato chips and thought of how adventurous I was, how bold.

The next morning was sunny by 4:30 AM. I was up early drinking coffee. By six I, Jerry, Andy, George and the rest of the crew were climbing into the side of a Sikorsky.

The trip in the old helicopter seemed to take a long time. We sat like tired troopers on our packs on the metal floor, not talking because of the noise. When we finally got out on the cold hillside with mountains rising behind it the silence rang in our ears.

Piles of gear lay everywhere. The two younger men I would be tenting with looked around with me.

"Pretty big camp," Wade said.

I nodded. "Bigger than the last one I was at."

Octave said, "There's gonna be some drinking tonight. Separate the sheep from the goats."

"What d'you mean?"

"The drinkers get fired. The rest of us stay."

That night, after we'd got our tent up and moved in, Octave sat with his legs crossed on his bunk and started muttering Hail Marys over a string of polished black beads.

Wade stared at him. "What you doing?"

"My rosary."

"What's that?"

"You don't know what a rosary is?"

"Uh uh."

"You ever go to church?"

"No."

Octave looked at me. I shrugged.

"I can't explain it," Octave said. "It's got to do with sins."

"Sins?"

"You know what a fucking sin is?"

"Yeah I know. I guess I do eh?" Wade had flushed. "Course I know what a sin is."

"What is it?"

"A sin is…." Wade's face and neck turned violently red. "It's bad."

Octave smiled. "You're right."

"Good."

After a minute Wade leaned forward, his face innocent again. "So what d'you do with the rosary?"

I get my sins forgiven."

"Who forgives them?"

"God."

"God?"

"That's right."

"Fuck, that's neat."

A few nights later, egged on by Wade, Octave told us about the saint he had adopted as his guardian.

"She lived in the middle ages," he said.

"How long ago was that?" Wade said.

Octave looked at me. "Five, six hundred years," I said.

"Wow," Wade said.

Octave nodded. "Long time ago. And I'll tell you eh, she had a hard fucking death." He was again sitting with his legs crossed on his cot, small, dark, with a missing front tooth and ratty hair that he picked at like a chimp. A tattoo of a snake on his left arm extended down to the back of his hand.

"What happened to her?" Wade said.

"What happened to her? She was burned to death. They piled wood under her and then they put gas on the wood and they lit it."

"They didn't have gas then," I said.

"Okay it wasn't gas. It was pitch. You know, like what seeps out of trees in the summer. It was that. They put that on the wood and they lit it. And then the fire burned her feet. She started screaming. She was howling."

"Jesus," Wade said.

"Yeah, she was on fire. She was smoking. It smelled like a barbecue."

"Fuck," Wade said.

"It gets worse. After a bit her face started to blister and her eyes popped out on their eyecords like fucking springs."

"Shit, man!" Wade half stood up.

Octave looked calmly at him. "She was in agony eh. She had no mouth any more to scream with. The rope burnt off and she moved her legs and arms up like this—" Octave demonstrated, pulling himself into the fetal position—"cause that's what you do when you get burnt that bad. And then at the end she was just a crisp eh. Just a little thing. Maybe two, three feet high. A crisp. With teeth in it."

"Fuck!"

Octave stopped and lay back on his cot with his legs still crossed. With his bare feet, he looked like a little yogi. He stretched his arms out behind his head and closed his eyes.

Wade stared at him. After a minute he said: "So what happened?"

Octave opened his eyes."You wanna know?"

"Yeah I wanna know."

"What d'you think, Bruce."

"You better tell us or he's gonna pop you."

"That's right you fucker. C'mon!"

"Okay." Octave sat up. He put his hands in his lap with their palms turned up. "Well, she burnt up," he said. "But then that night, everyone's gone to bed, one old man he comes down to the square where they burnt her. And there she is."

He looked at Wade. "She's lying there naked. Her tits are perfect with their pink nipples. Her eyelids are shut. Perfect. Her whole body. None of her has stayed burnt, not even her little toe nails. And later, when they buried her, she didn't decay like an ordinary body. She smelled like roses. And even now, her body is perfect. That's why she's a saint."

A few days later it snowed.

Looking out with me from our tent, Wade grinned. "This is fucking great eh? Snow in July. Hey Octave, isn't this great?"

Octave sat in the tent behind us on a round of log. He was sharpening an axe. He had placed the axe so that the axe handle was under one knee and the axe head on top of the other knee. With the axe firmly in place, gripped between his knees, he'd taken a flat file and was now strongly stroking the blade, leaving a shiny regular path about a half inch wide along the edge. As we watched, he turned the axe over and did the same thing on the other side.

106

When he was finished he felt the blade on the ball of his thumb. "Calice de calice," he said. "That's fucking sharp."

Wade said, "What's that: 'Calice de calice.'"

"That's French."

"I know it's French, asshole. What does it mean?"

"It means...." Octave shook his head. "No, it sounds stupid in English."

"Octave, c'mon, what does it mean?"

"It means chalice of chalices."

"That is stupid."

"Yeah but that's because French swearwords aren't like English eh. When French swear it's always about God. They blaspheme God."

"That's neat." Wade stepped over to Octave. "Let me feel it."

Octave handed him the axe. Wade felt the blade with his thumb. "Calice de calice, that is fucking sharp."

"Your pronunciation is pitiful."

"Well then teach me."

"You wanna learn French?"

"Yeah."

That evening, Octave taught Wade and me to swear in French. We learned tabernac and tabernouche and calice and others too.

"The worst one?" he said in answer to Wade's question. "The worst is moitse Chriss."

"What does it mean?"

"It means, 'Go to hell, Christ.'"

"Moitse Chriss."

"No. Say it like this. Moitse Chriss."

"Okay. Moitse Chriss."

"That's better. Moitse Chriss."

"Moitse Chriss."

"Good going man," Octave said. "You got it. Now you're

fucking tough."

Under my breath, I said, "Moitse Chriss."

The next morning I got up in the dark as usual and went over to the cook tent to make the coffee and lay the tables. It was about four-thirty a.m. I worked in perfect silence, my shadow doubled by the light coming from the incandescent bulbs strung under the canvas. As I worked I thought of Wade and Octave, the innocence of the one, the cynical eyes of the other.

And then, as I did almost every day, I imagined Cate arriving. A helicopter had landed in the dark. Cate stepped down from it and ran across the hillside to the lit-up cook tent. She tentatively opened the flap; she came in.

"Cate. What are you doing here?"

"I came to see you."

"How come?"

No. Not how come.

"I came to see you."

"Good."

Her cheeks are pink from the cold. "I spent all my money to make this trip."

"Why?"

"I want to marry you."

'Interesting."

"What d'you think?"

"This is a bit unexpected."

"You don't want me?"

She undoes the top button of her shirt and walks up to me. I look at her eyes, her heavy hair. She touches me and I feel breathless with happiness.

I finished my chores. Outside the light was breaking. I went out to watch the dawn. The sky was becoming a perfect blue. A clean fresh wind blew. I shivered in my jean jacket, eyes watering. The sun spread a bar of incandescence on the high mountains in the southwest. Slowly, walking toward the light, I hiked up into the alpine meadows. And then in the grass, almost underfoot, I saw a ptarmigan. It moved toward me, flapping its wings, getting my attention; then it started to run, hoping I would go after it. I looked closely where I had first seen it and saw a clutch of small speckled blue eggs there in the grass.

When I straightened up twenty or thirty caribou were passing in front of me, not more than ten yards away. They moved slowly, dropping their heads to eat, then walking on. They moved across the hillside, and I watched them until they had passed.

VI

Toward the end of July I received a letter from Jeannine, written in a quick, round hand.

Dear Bruce,

How are you doing? Are you working hard? I have a lot of news but I don't know where to start. Ha ha.

I guess I'll start with the news about Alistair. Some guys came around asking for him so I went up to have a look and he wasn't in his room but two girls were in his bed. They were naked and trampy looking, with really pimply faces. They laughed at me and one of them lifted one of her breasts toward me. I don't know how they got there! I had a weird thought that maybe Alistair let them in on a ladder. The other girl said Alistair isn't around.

The house got raided about a week ago, the cops made a complete mess. But they didn't find anything. It freaked me out. Alex, the guy who is staying in your room, is dealing coke. Ray said he told you about that but I don't know if he told you it really scares me. Also I don't like him, he's way too tough and you know Ray he's such a soft touch and he thinks Alex is okay. But we've got criminals coming around now. A couple of days ago there was a guy who was passed out in the bathtub from using too much heroin.

The day the police raided the house they had been observing us from across the street for maybe two weeks,

110

*then they moved in and like I say they overturned every-
thing. All the dresser drawers were pulled open and everything was out on the floor. It made me cry when I saw it.
But they didn't find Ray's stash.*

*And the other thing is that now Lillian's gone again.
Moose just mopes around. I don't think I can live in the
house anymore. I need to find another place to live but I
don't know how to tell Ray. Anyway I'm sorry about all
this bad news! I hope you're doing well up North. Write to
me with all your news!*

*Love & hugs & kisses,
Jeannine.*

I was thinking about Jeannine's letter and wondering how to
reply when Octave pulled it out of my hand and started reading
it. "Two naked girls in one bed! Man you got wild friends!"

"Give me that."

He stepped away, grinning, and held the letter out in front of
him. "Hey Wade, listen to this. 'They were naked and trampy
looking. They laughed at me and one of them lifted her legs in the
air and slowly moved her hand over her little cuntlet. The other
one started licking her tit—'"

"Give me that you bugger."

"Ha ha ha! Bruce you get these hot fucking letters." He
handed the letter back, pulled up a round of log and sat by my
cot. "So what's that all about?"

"Why should I tell you?"

"Cause I'm curious."

"Yeah, you're curious all right."

Wade watched us, waiting to see the show.

"Sounds like things aren't so good," Octave said after a bit.

"They're all right. The place I was living in is having problems."

"That's in Vancouver?"

"Yeah."

Octave waited for me to say more. Then he nodded. "Well what about you Wade? You got a letter. What does it say."

Wade hunched his shoulders, suddenly shy. "It's from my mom."

"And?"

"It's from my mom." He looked at Octave. "Don't you get letters?"

"Me? No. Fuck."

I said, "No letters at all?"

"Nope."

"What about your mom and dad."

"Ha. My mom, I havent seen her since I was fucking nine years old. And my dad, fuck him."

"That doesn't sound so good."

"It's all right."

"You don't get along with your dad?"

"Ha ha ha. You kidding?"

"How come?"

"He's Indian eh. He's always pissed off. And he's a goddam liar." After a moment he added, "Goddamn Indians, they're all liars."

"You think so?"

"I should know. I been around them all my life."

Wade leaned forward on his cot, his hands clasped between his knees. "Yeah but Octave. If your dad's an Indian then you're an Indian. And you're not a liar."

"How do you know."

"They're not all liars."

"You don't know what you're talking about."

"I know you," Wade said.

"What do you know about me? You don't know nothing."

Octave picked up a needle and thread and one of his slippers and sat on another round of log under the light of the electric bulb strung up at the tent's ceiling. A ruddier light came from the wood stove in the centre of the floor. He held the slipper loosely in his hand and stared at the fire. Shadows flickered on his face. After a while he shook his head. Then he pulled a pack of Export A's out his shirt pocket and held it out to Wade. "Here. Have a smoke. You started smoking, right?"

"Yeah. Thanks." Wade got up from his cot and went over to Octave. Octave pushed the package open and held it out. "Take two," he said.

"Thanks."

"You too, Bruce." He held the package out to me.

They were rollies, beautifully made.

For a while I smoked and watched my two tentmates. Wade was sitting on the edge of his cot, gingerly smoking and watching Octave sew the slipper, a beaded mocassin trimmed with wool.

After a minute's silence he said, "You'd wear those things into the bush if you could."

Octave looked up at him and grinned. "You know what, they're more comfortable than your mom's kiss on your bum when you're a baby."

I laughed. Octave looked at me. "Hey you know your partner Jerry, he must have got a pretty bad letter."

"Why d'you say that?"

"I was in their tent talking to em and he was curled up like a fucking little kid on his cot."

I looked at him. "Well, Jerry's a nervous guy. He's pretty shy you know."

"I know that. This wasn't that."

The next day Octave again mentioned Jerry's grief. And that evening I found out what he meant.

Just after supper, Andy stuck his head in our tent. "Hey Bruce, you doing anything?"

"No."

"Well then come on over to the map tent. We'll show you where we've been blasting."

Andy and George were explaining to me how the radio telephone worked when Jerry came in.

"I wanna make a call," he said.

"Jerry, we're showing Bruce the equipment," George said.

"So I can't use it?"

"No. That's not it." He smiled and touched his tentmate's shoulder. "You know, you just made a call yesterday. You made two calls."

"So?"

"Those calls are expensive. Gonna use up all your money."

"My money isn't it."

Andy said, "Jerry, day before yesterday you made—what. Three calls? You're only gonna get hurt. That's no good."

"I gotta talk to her."

George shook his head. "Okay. You go ahead. She don't wanna talk to you."

Waiting for the connection, Jerry stood hunched forward over the radio telephone, his left hand pressed across his chest. I turned and pretended to be looking at a map.

"Hi, it's me," Jerry said. He scratched his head. "Yah, I know I just called you."

He bent forward, listening.

"Yah, I know."

He listened, shook his head.

"No, no, please listen." He turned and looked at the tent wall. "Please, I have to talk to you."

I looked down at the map, no longer wishing to observe him.

"Oh ma petite, why, why, why do you talk like this."

I stood still.

"Oh god. Please don't say that...don't do that."

I looked. He was blinking his eyes.

"No. That's not true. I love you, don't you know?" While I watched he started to cry. "Please baby tell me you love me eh. Please. Please."

I looked down. The glamour that had filled the tent five minutes before had vanished. I had had—in the way of a young man, my body prickling with shame—a moment of understanding. I understood that Jerry was maimed; he was in the bush for a reason.

A few days later, while we were packing up, Andy came to our tent alone. His face was impassive. "Bruce, you got a call."

It was Lillian. Her voice was deeper and softer than I remembered. She said, "Eh Bruce, how are you doing?"

"I'm good, Lillian. I'm fine. How did you get this number?"

"Jeannine gave it to me. No—she told me the name of the outfit, and I asked Moose about em. He knew who they were."

"Okay. So—how are you doing?"

"Oh, so so. Not great. I don't want to embarrass you—I wouldn't have called eh—but you should know." She stopped speaking. I held my hand up to my other ear, trying to hear if she was saying anything through the background noise.

"Know what? What is it, Lillian?"

Her voice was small in the crackle. "Alistair died."

"What?"

"Yah, he died. I am so sorry to tell you."

"How did he die?"

"I don't know all the details. But he was coming home from a beer parlour with some other kids. I guess the driver was drunk eh. And the car they were in went out of control. I guess it hit a lamp post."

"Oh boy."

"I am so sorry. I know what a good friend he was to you."

"Do you know who was driving?"

"Yeah." She made a noise, a gulping, slurping sound. I pressed the receiver against my ear, trying to listen.

"Who was it?"

"That's the problem."

"What d'you mean?"

"I guess it was Ray."

"Ray?"

"Yeah. It was Ray."

"Lillian, are you okay?"

"Oh shit. Bruce, I gotta hang up. Okay? I gotta go."

I went out of the radio tent and walked into the night. I smoked and walked around in the dark, looking at the mountains and up at the stars. A bleak excitement took hold of me. I felt a need for action. I needed to do something. I needed to make a move.

The Sikorsky came down out of the blue sky, its rotors thundering. Andy took me aside. "Okay. Now about Jerry and George. I want you to chaperone them. They're gonna need taking care of. Don't let them drink eh."

"Okay."

"Watch them like a hawk. I'm telling you."

"Okay." I grinned. He didn't grin back. "I'm not kidding."

I wasn't careful enough. We waited at the Watson Lake air strip about fifteen minutes; in those fifteen minutes George somehow managed to get a bottle of whiskey and to get himself and Jerry drunk.

On the plane the two men turned mean. They shouted at the stewardess.

She said to me, "Sir, you gotta calm them down."

"You hear that, George?" I said. "You gotta calm down."

"Fuck off," George said. He swiveled his head toward me slowly. His eyes looked boiled. "Who the fuck're you? You my dad? Huh? You fucking cocksucker. Don't tell me to calm down."

I said, "Come on, Jerry, help me here."

"Help yourself," Jerry said.

"George, I'm not your dad. I'm just this kid Andy asked to keep an eye out in case you guys got loaded. That's all."

"You think I'm loaded?"

"What d'you think?"

"I'm stinkin fuckin drunk. That's what I am."

Jerry laughed. So did George. Finally they both quieted down and went to sleep.

When we arrived in Vancouver the two men said goodbye to me. Jerry shook my hand without speaking, clasping it firmly, looking at me with his simple eyes. George touched my shoulder. "We'll see you around, Bruce. Don't you worry."

"I'll see you two," I said, and hoped that I would. I didn't know that the people of my youth would vanish without even leaving behind ghosts.

The next day I called the house.

Jeannine answered. When she heard it was me she started crying. "I'm not living here anymore. It's too awful. I just happened to be in getting my things."

"Is Ray still there?"

"No. He moved out."

"Where's he staying?"

"He's got a place of his own. It's a basement suite. It's not great, but."

"Yeah." I paused. "You got the address?"

"Yes, I do. Its 238 Princess. It's around the back. Bruce, you should go see him."

"Yeah….Has he got a phone?"

"Yeah, but don't call him. He might not answer. But you should go see him. It'll do him good. Just don't call him. Just go."

That night I bought an umbrella at a store near the Niagara and walked in the pouring rain east on Hastings to Princess Street. The 200 block was down toward the water. My outside arm and pantlegs were wet with rain when I reached an old stucco house that had a wood shed in the front yard. I went around the back. Down two slick black steps a plywood door with a strip of leather hanging from it stood open a few inches.

I pushed the door wide and stepped into the basement. I stood in the gloom for a moment looking around, then knocked on the inside door.

"Who's there?"

"Hey Ray. It's me, Bruce."

"Bruce. Come on in. The door's open."

I went in.

Ray was lying on his side in the dark. A bed on the floor. His hair was lanky with grease and there was a huge bruise on his cheek. He was smoking, placing the cigarette in a finicky way between puffy lips.

He said, "Hey Bruce," and I saw that his two front teeth had been knocked out. I sat on the floor by the bed. Ray sat up tailor-style and held up his hand. We shook.

He said, "Here, let me light some candles. The bulb doesn't work."

He lit four or five candles that were stuck in their own wax on the floor. Then he sat back on the bed. "You wanna smoke up?"

"Sure."

He got out some hashish and a small pipe and we each took two tokes. Then he put the pipe away and looked at me. "I guess you want to know what happened."

"Sure, if you want to tell me."

He nodded. "Yeah I do."

For a long while he was silent. Then he began to talk, speaking in a monotone, low, soft, almost rapturous. "Okay. We were at the Anchor. I guess maybe there was about eight of us. We were drinking pretty good. Then we went to the Egmont. We were drinking some more."

He paused. "Then we left. A bunch of us. I was driving, Alistair sat next to me, then Dave."

"Who's Dave?"

"One of the new guys at the house."

"Okay."

"The car was packed. I remember we were laughing and shouting. We turned to go up to Hastings. We were going pretty fast and this other car came at us."

"He came at you."

"I don't know entirely about that bit. Just all at once there was this car. It was just coming right toward us."

"Huh."

"Yeah. So I swerved. The car goes out of control. We're flying across the sidewalk and then whump. Huge fucking noise. We hit a light post. Bent it right over. My head slammed into the dash. But Alistair's head got cracked open."

"Right."

"Yeah." Ray shuddered. "I come to and look over and Alistair's head is just wrenched over. Just like twisted right over. It looked really bad."

"Right." Then I added, "It must have scared you."

"Yeah."

I looked at him. "You need to get your teeth fixed man."

"No."

"What d'you mean, no."

"I mean no."

119

I was silent for a moment. "Ray, that's—"

"You know what, he's dead now eh."

"Ray, he chose to be in the car too."

He didn't respond. Instead he said, almost idly, "Just like my dad."

"What d'you mean?"

"That's how he died. And he killed my mom too. What an idiot."

Later we talked about the days that were coming up.

I said, "How're things with Jeannine?"

"I'm seeing her. Man, I love her. But I'm too fucked up." He picked up the matches from the floor and lit one of the candles that had gone out. "Anyway, yeah, she's gonna go back to Nanaimo and stay with her mom for a bit."

"You're gonna miss her."

"Yeah. You know it." And all at once he grinned, that grin that was so sweet and wide and that to me was the street itself. And now, whenever I think about that period of my life, I just have to remember Ray's grin for it all to come back.

4. Odlum Drive

I

Shorter days now. Rain beat on the window of my room in the Niagara Hotel; wet air blew in the few inches the window was cracked open. The room faced Burrard Inlet, and often I pulled up a chair to feel the wet air on my face and look out at seagulls flying across the sky.

Patterns in the chill air, appearing then vanishing. Like a heiromancer, I seemed to see in them the secret of my friend's death.

One bright cold November morning I woke full of anger and washed and dressed and walked quickly down the stairs to the Sportsman's Cafe and ordered a coffee to go. Blowing on it and gulping it down, I stepped through the cigarette smoke out into the cold and walked down the frosty sidewalk to the bus stop on Hastings.

The house on Adanac Street reeked of marijuana. But nobody was in the living room. I called upstairs. No one there. I went down the dark hall. I entered the kitchen.

It was full of smoke. Six or seven strangers sat around the

table—a table I knew well, rectangular, painted blue, the paint peeling off on the corners—playing poker and smoking huge marijuana cigarettes made with twists of newspaper.

I saw that the marijuana came from a brick-shaped kilogram that had been opened onto the table. And then I realized that one of the strangers was my brother Mike.

He had followed my sister Marie-Claire up to Vancouver when my family moved to Portland. And after I moved out of the Adanac house, he'd started to come over, visiting my friends and smoking marijuana and hashish. But I hadn't expected to see him.

An older man in his late twenties or early thirties was leaning over the kitchen counter with a rolled-up paper tube in his mouth. He was sucking up hashish smoke from a piece of hashish that had been placed on a kitchen knife heated redhot on the stove. He didn't have a shirt on; his upper body was muscular. He wore tight jeans and heavy boots and when he sat back down the younger men playing poker deferred to him.

I stood there for a moment in the kitchen entrance watching this.

Finally I said, "Mike, what are you doing here? It's not even noon. Jesus Christ."

I walked toward him.

The older man without the shirt said, "You Mike's brother?"

"Yeah, I am. Come on, Mike. Let's get out of here."

"Let him finish the game."

I turned toward the man. "Hey. Excuse me, okay? This is none of your business, right? C'mon, Mike, I'll buy you lunch."

My brother got up, red-eyed and smiling nervously. We went outside, into the bright cold day. We started walking up Adanac.

After a while I said, "Where d'you usually eat?"

"There's a place on Commercial…."

As we walked Mike talked about the great coffee you could buy on Commercial and how the guys had filled the fridge with a bag of really good beans. I thought: He's trying to impress me, trying to be one of the boys. I listened impatiently. And then I recognized how much he wanted to please me; and my anger drained into a pool of sadness.

Not long after that I started working in Revelstoke. I lived with a family of railroad workers in a small room that on hot days was like an oven. I worked in Revelstoke Park; and I dressed like the railroad workers, like them carrying my lunch pail tied to a piece of thick string slung over my shoulders and like them wearing dark blue denim and a heavy checked black and blue wool jacket. I was getting to know them, and I felt a kind of peace.

Early one morning in late August when I was walking to work I saw Don Ross walking toward me. The sky overhead was pure blue; the shadows of a slow-moving train of boxcars rippled over the grasses that grew along the tracks.

A beautiful morning. Yet I felt dismay. My calm disappeared. Everything I'd been seeking to avoid now stood in front of me.

His hair was very long. He was wearing a scarf or a tie through the belt loops of his pants. He smiled and came up close and put his hand on my shoulder and looked at me. "Well, well. The workingman." I could smell his breath. "How're you doing?"

"I'm fine."

"Good."

We looked at each other.

I said, "What're you doing here?"

"We're playing at the Regent. I'm just headed there for breakfast. Want to come along?"

I shook my head. "I have to go to work."

"Too bad. So what are *you* doing here, besides working?"

"That's it."

"Okay," he said.

"And you?"

"I'm at UBC. Just about finished. One more semester. Then I'm going into law."

"That's great."

"I think it is." He stepped toward me and fingered the string that held my lunch pail. "You've become a railroad man."

"I guess I have."

"Good." He held out his hand. "I'm off. Who knows—maybe I'll see you again."

"Maybe."

I watched him walk down the road.

After a minute I stepped across the tracks toward the highway. And as I walked onto the highway, thinking of Don, of how he was moving beyond me and how I would have to stop considering him a friend, I said out loud: "I've been here too long," and the sudden panic I felt made me walk faster, my heart pounding, as if there was somewhere I had to get to but I had all but run out of time.

That fall I went back to school. In December it snowed. And one night not long after the snow started I and my new friend and roommate Paul Sante arrived home covered with snow to find that Rufus Zill had unpacked his last box. Seven months later Rufus would leave for England and Paul would follow him; but for now the three of us were living together in a townhouse apartment at the bottom of Burnaby Mountain near Lougheed.

The communal part of the apartment—living room and dining room—is furnished a la mode: patio furniture in the dining room—a round white metal table complete with umbrella and four plastic lawn chairs—and in the living room a foamie covered by a dirty green sleeping bag that has a print of wagon wheels and cowboys inside it. In the middle of the room lies a pile of books that might have been dumped off the back of a truck—about 200 SFU library books heaped up on the matted wall-to-wall carpet.

When we walk in, brushing the snow off our coats, Rufus is sitting like a tailor on the hall floor. Empty boxes, still carrying a trace of their rich BC Liquor Store smell, are piled up at his feet. He reaches one arm behind him and shakes an outstretched finger. "Round the corner."

We go round the corner. Hanging from the living room wall is a tacked-up white slip with two pencils stuck in the brassiere part to mimic breasts.

"I've also added a few more books to the pile," Rufus says.

In fact, maybe three-quarters of the books in the living room have been taken out by him. Like Paul and me, Rufus is studying English at SFU. He's Jewish, a skinny twenty-one-year-old orphan who wears black shoes and bluejeans and white shirts with the cuffs undone. Before he moved in with us he stayed with an aunt at a small house in West Vancouver. When I went to visit him one day he was playing Gregorian chant so loud I heard it a block down the street. Standing beside him in his room where he was writing something, I said, "D'you think you should turn it down?"

"No." He didn't look up from the sheet of paper he was writing on.

"What about your aunt?"

"I hope it deafens her, the ugly cunt."

Upstairs in my bedroom, I don't turn on the light. Through the little window I can see darkness, falling snow and the faint lights of Lumberland on the Lougheed Highway. I walk in the night luminescence through a litter of papers over to the desk I've made of a five-dollar Lumberland door placed on two old filing cabinets. Three library books are neatly stacked in the desk's centre. A note is taped to the top one.

I turn on the desk lamp. The note reads: "You might like these. Then again you might not. Rufus." The books are Robert Warshow's *The Immediate Experience,* R. P. Blackmur's *Form and Value in Modern Poetry* and Walter Benjamin's *Illuminations.*

I leaf through the books. After a while I sit down and pull the typewriter from the back of the desk toward the front. I stare at it. Then I roll in a sheet of paper. I set the left and right margins in a little closer than usual. And for the twentieth or thirtieth time, I type across the top of the page:

> *The Escape Artist*
> *Reflections on Robinson Crusoe*

Five lines down and five spaces in I type the Roman numeral "I"; two lines below that I once more start my first sentence.

Barry Strauss's American Lit class has had a room change. We don't know if we're going the right way. It's snowing again, and the lights are flickering on and off in the corridors. We walk quickly, smoking as we walk. I feel excited: Paul has persuaded Rufus to sit in on the class, our favourite. When we finally enter the room and face the other students sitting around the big seminar table (the flourescent light harsh and momentarily disorienting after the darkness out in the hall), I'm so keyed up I have to frown to control myself.

A minute later Strauss walks in. He stands at the end of the table and looks down. He puts his scarred, multi-buckled, black leather briefcase on the table. He slowly opens it. He takes out his papers and books; he arranges them. Then he pushes his tinted glasses into his wooly hair and looks at us with small, naked, suffering eyes. He's a little over five feet tall, obese, and tonight as usual wears tight pants in the early 70s style and platform shoes

126

and a tight velvet sports coat.

He stares briefly at Rufus. "What are you doing here?"

"I'm with them."

He looks at Paul and me. "So you brought the bugger. Okay. Welcome to the class. Feel free to join in."

Ten minutes later Paul and I are arguing with Strauss about Saul Bellow's novel *Herzog*. The rest of the class watches and listens.

"What about Whitman then?" Strauss says. "Is he a sentimental klutz too?"

Rufus, who's been sitting slumped in his chair, not talking, now straightens up. "No—Whitman has a formal verbal energy that radicalizes everything he writes about. Even when he writes about 'the lilacs that last in the dooryard bloomed' there's nothing inspissated in his work."

"He's not modern though. He's an optimistic writer," Ann Donet says. Her mild white face is attentive.

Rufus turns to her. He waves his cigarette. "He *is* modern. His linguistic sensibility is modern."

"But can't one distinguish between temperament and use of language?"

"Sure. *You* can distinguish. But posterity doesn't. All posterity cares about is linguistic energy. That's why we're talking about him."

Rufus and Paul and I are sitting together in one of our rare Canlit classes. It's a big class, held in a big lecture theatre, AQ 9008. We're sitting up at the back. The professor down below—red cheeks, soft black leather jacket—is discussing Margaret Atwood's *Lady Oracle*. Then he stops. "The real *problem* with the novel, of course, is that Atwood is being cruelly unfair to obese women."

Rufus laughs, a loud bark. The professor looks up.

"You have a comment up there?"

Loudly Rufus says, "It's nonsense to talk about Atwood being unfair. Her book is a satire."

"So you think it's all right for her to joke about fat people?"

"Yeah, I do. Don't you?"

"No, I don't."

"Don't ever write a satire then."

Pub night at SFU. The packed basement reeks of sweat. Boys with slitted red eyes clomp in front of girls whose breasts swing loose in their shirts and who'll soon get loose enough to dance with anyone. Rufus and Paul and I have been drinking steadily and arguing about Canadian writing.

"Cuntlit, that's what we need," Paul says.

"Fuck off." I've become sullen.

Paul grins at me. "Ah yes, Canadian novels by gar. *Tabernac the Toque. Dogsled Days*—"

"It's our country—"

"*Bushed and Buggered.*" This is from Rufus. He sticks a cigarette in his left nostril. "Look." He tilts his head back and carefully lifts his cup. "I can smoke and drink beer at the same time."

He takes the cigarette out of his nose and offers it to me. "Want a drag? By the way, only an imbecile reads Canlit."

"Then I'm an imbecile."

He looks at me. He must see something in my flushed face besides the beer. "No you're not." His voice quickens, and a tone enters it which, like a ray of light, allows me to see into his heart. "Bruce, I apologize for what I just said. It was stupid, and I hope you'll forgive me."

Later Rufus will drop English and get his degree in engineering. By the time he's forty-eight he'll be a millionaire, having patented a way to reduce the information needed to send a digitized movie over the internet. But now he's our friend.

II

The old bus station on Dunsmuir Street no longer exists. But you can still feel something of its atmosphere in the stinking washroom in the Main Street train terminal, where old men groan in the stalls, the sounds echoing in the tiled room.

It's from that smelly and no-longer-existing station that I leave in the spring for Revelstoke. When I come back at the end of the summer my sleeping bag smells like a camp fire. The last notation in my bankbook tells me (in a small neat hand, in blue ink) that I've saved 3873 dollars. I'm exuberant. But where to live? Rufus has decided to spend the winter in Montreal and Paul's staying at his parents'. Studying the student housing ads in the big concourse at SFU, I rock back and forth, the soles of my cowboy boots squeaking on the black rubber.

One sign catches my eye: "Roommate wanted—English student preferred." I write the address on my hand. The card has a phone number, but I want to just present myself, not call ahead.

The house is down by the docks, on Odlum Drive. It's old, stuccoed, but with a noticeable touch: next to it, separated from it by a tangle of blackberry bushes, stands a wooden building whose apartments seem to have been rented out to whores: dozens of white condoms, obviously thrown from the apartment building's windows, hang from the brambles in the sun. The picket fence sags. The old concrete walkway is almost lost in the kneehigh grass. The stink from a chicken processing plant a few blocks away makes me lift my arm to my nose as I walk up the steps to the porch.

I knock on one of the door's glass panes. A moment later the door opens and a mountain man so big he fills the doorway stares at me. Slippers bulge on his feet; his jeans—old man jeans—are greyer than ordinary Levis. Even through his beard I can see the frown that tightens his mouth.

Can I help you?"

"I hope so. I'm here about the ad for a roommate."

His eyes change. The stern giant standing in front of me turns into a smiling child.

"Great! Come on in!"

We pass through a cavelike room that smells of pancakes. Walking behind him, I notice that this huge man has the look of the congenital bachelor with a paunch who moves along with his bum stuck out and his legs spread slightly apart. As we walk up the stairs and along a hall past bedrooms painted orange, we talk.

"I'm Gene."

"I'm Bruce."

"You a writer?"

"I'm a fire fighter."

"Well, that's not bad."

In the kitchen Gene calls out: "Hey, Popeye!" And a minute later an incarnation of Vancouver's hippie milieu walks into the room. He's wearing only a pair of dress slacks. Flabby shoulders and arms are patterned with chevrons of black hair, and the heavy stomach pushes aggressively out. The slacks are set below that stomach and are much too long. They bunch up around his feet, so that I see only the dirty toes with black hairs on their tops.

Gene and I sit at the kitchen table watching him. Gene says, "Popeye, meet our new roommate. He's a writer."

"No shit." Popeye goes over to the kitchen counter and picks up an opened-up milk carton. He sniffs at it. Then he leans back against the counter with the palms of his hands on the counter's edge and stares at me.

"What d'you write?"

"I don't write anything. I fight fires."

"That a new form of literature? Something avant garde there?"

"Nope. Just work."

"Sounds dull."

"I guess it is."

"You ever read Levi-Strauss?"

"I've read *Sad Tropics.*"

"What about Lew Welch?"

"Yeah, I've read him."

"What about Gilbert Sorrentino?"

Now I'm staring at him. Gene stands up. "Sure he's a writer. He's putting you on. Come on, let's have a coffee."

Popeye rubs his face. He walks over to the fridge and opens it and looks in. Then he turns and says: "You ever read Merleau-Ponty?"

"Sure."

"Good."

Both Gene and Popeye have poems coming out in *The Capilano Review.* This excites me. But I don't mention it to Paul or write about it to Rufus. We're intensely competitive, and what matters to us most we don't discuss.

All our talk about books—it was so fierce because it's a surrogate for achievement. We walked down Holdom arguing in loud voices, sometimes even shouting; but if anyone we know writes something about their actual life, it disturbs us. Better to stay with the talk!

Here on Odlum Drive, though, in the gloomy hall and the living room downstairs, something like a real literary world presses in: paintings by Bill Bissett, photographs of Jack Spicer and Robert Duncan, and framed poems by Fielding Dawson, Charles

Olson and Fred Wah. A black-and-white street map of Vancouver hangs in Popeye's room, and a huge map of BC curls on the wall above Gene's bed. But it's the dozens of local chapbooks that fill Popeye's heavy shelves that most give me a sense that I've entered another world so far as writing is concerned.

My own shelves are meagre. They're two metal strips screwed vertically into the bedroom wall with brackets inserted into the strips and boards on the brackets—light, tight-assed shelves on which I place my conventional books: Benjamin, Kafka, Barthes.

So far I've been happy with these books. But now, no sooner are they up than they seem different than they did before. All at once they appear separate from the world around me. They belong to another universe entirely than the one that holds the chapbooks and pamphlet-type books that fill Popeye's shelves.

Those books are connected to the local world almost by an umbilical cord. When I leaf through them (surreptitiously— Popeye has to be out before I'll enter his room), the things I notice—the dry, ragged-edged paper of the covers, the staples that held the pamphlets together, the typefaces and page sizes, and especially the uncertain language that makes the poems seem like personal letters —all this gives a feeling of fluidity and possibility to Popeye's shelves that's missing from my own collection.

My books are cut off from the world in which people grope for words. They're achieved things. The barrier between them and the language I hear and speak every day seems like a steel wall. But when I open Popeye's books and read a good line, it's as if between the world of the Hastings bus and the world of words a hot spark has jumped.

Gene writes longhand. He comes up with a few sentences at a time, lying on his bed after supper drinking beer. When I look for the first time into his room I see sheets of paper on the bed, beer bottles, bowls that've been filled with ice cream, and so many shirts and pairs of pants and underwear it's as if a bag of laundry has been emptied across the floor.

Among this detritus Gene lies on the bed with his whalelike back propped against the wall, newly shorn of his beard, his broad baby face naked-looking in the evening sunlight shining on it.

"Wanna hear something great?" he says.

"Sure."

Gene loves to recite literature. In fact, reading to others is for him such an intense pleasure that it seems to me a good part of his life has become a search for occasions on which he can indulge in it.

"Okay! All right! Good!" he says now.

He sits up higher on his bed. He lights a cigarette and takes a long drag. He stares at the book in his hand. Then he starts, sentences that it takes me a while to realize are from Milton's *Paradise Lost.*

He reads slowly, one hand marking in the air the prosaic counterstresses to Milton's five-beat lines. Occasionally he emphasizes or pauses on a word.

The poem seems to enlarge the sunlit room and extend it into space. I sit on the bedroom floor with my back against the wall smoking and listening. A pair of Gene's underwear lies inches from my stretched-out leg. Light from the west window comes in and lights up our cigarette smoke. I smell the acrid wheat smell from the grain elevators down on the docks, the sickening smell of the chickens, the beef stroganoff Gene made for dinner.

I listen for ten minutes. Finally I stand up. Gene keeps reading. I leave the room and stand outside the door leaning against a wall. Still Gene reads, coming out into the hall with me. I slip into my room. Gene keeps reading even then, standing outside my door, and for many minutes I listen to him as I lie on my bed in the bright evening light, my hands clasped on my chest and my eyes closed.

"Gene's editing a magazine?" Paul looks up from his coffee; this interests him.

"Yeah."

"What's it called?"

"*Ghost Horse.* He's taken it over from David Brown."

"Is it any good?"

"I think so."

"You think he'd take something by me?"

"He might."

Paul sips his coffee; considers. "What kind of reputation does it have?"

"Pretty good, I think. There's always writers coming by."

"What kind of writers?"

"Poets."

"Poets."

"Yeah."

"What are they like? Are they any good?"

"Yeah, some are good. A lot of them've come down from the Interior. They like to act tough."

Paul grins. "Are they tough?"

"Naw. They're aristocrats. They're elegant. They have white faces and they dramatize every fucking thing that happens to them. And man they're cruel."

"What d'you mean."

"I mean they're cruel. They're fantastically self-absorbed. You know, I think they get off on hurting each other."

One afternoon I sit in the living room with three of the poets: Gene and David Brown and Al Massie. Brown has had six poems printed in the last issue of *Ghost Horse.* He effortlessly commands our attention. He's a short man with a beard and a clean upper lip and an air of sadness that isolates him from the rest of us. He's talking about his recent travels. As he talks I feel he's withholding everything that mattered to him.

"So in this cabin, a hundred miles outside Terrace." He stops, considering it. "I found this thing."

He smokes.

"Tell us," Gene says.

"Bill Bissett's copy of the *Cantos.*"

Massie, leaning forward, his arms on his knees, looks at him. "Far out."

"It's autographed and slightly foxed." Brown exhales through his nose. "I suppose it's worth something."

Massie stares at him. Brown stares back. Massie looks down. Then he looks up and says, "What d'you think of Bissett? You think he's any good? I'm not too sure about his latest stuff. I think—"

"What are you talking about."

Embarrassment floods Massie. His face reddens as if congested with drink.

One evening while we're having supper Gene says: "Last pub night everyone was saying we ought to have a halloween party."

"Here in the house?"

"Why not?"

"How many people you think'll come."

"Everybody's gonna come. I'll bet you a hundred people show up."

Dense fog Halloween day. By six o'clock the streetlights are cottony globes. Coming down the sidewalk from school I can smell the gunpowder stink of firecrackers. The firecrackers pop off in strings in the dark. Kids run through the thicker fog of firecracker smoke carrying pillowcases and paper bags, the older boys and girls with masks on, the younger ones dressed in costumes that in the dark make them seem like small creatures out of some fairy-tale that's escaped from the pages of its book.

By nine the poets are streaming through the door. Robin Hood and Marion in green and yellow leather jerkins; two Strawberries; Beauty and the Beast. Watching their glitter and dash, excitement sweeps through me. I'm grinning, and have to restrain myself from laughing out loud.

I feel like the roommate; and to get over the feeling I pour a glass of whiskey and drink half of it. In waves, sixty or so students I recognize from SFU, students of the poets, enter the house—handsome people, the boys with thick dark hair and magnificent coats, the girls with glossy cheeks.

But they're remote. They adore their teachers, with an adoration that leaves no room for more robust emotions. They don't talk to each other; instead they wander the halls with drinks in their hands. Some step timidly into the bedroom where Gene and another poet are lying on Gene's bed listening to the baseball game being broadcast on the radio; and some, waiting to be noticed, stand by the couch where two SFU poet-professors (Rufus, who detests them, calls them the gurus) are holding court.

But whenever the students say a few words, they're either ignored or stared at; and eventually, painfully self-conscious, they go back to wandering.

Soon the house is filled with bored students. Then, glamour: two SFU stars walk in. Sharon Fawcett arrives first, smiling radiantly; minutes later Brian Fawcett enters the house with his new girlfriend. Sharon and Brian had a passionate marriage; it inspired gossip; now it's over; and maybe as a result, both of them have become fluent, Brian writing short stories and poems that are so fierce he's getting attention all across town, and Sharon publishing critical essays that are the talk of the English department.

Brian and his companion go into the bedroom to lie out with Gene; and Sharon walks into the packed living room, where the gurus, shouting with delight, move to make room on the couch.

Coming out of the bathroom a bit later I see Brian, holding a cigarette and a glass of whiskey, pass Sharon in the hall.

"How are you doing?" he says.

"I'm doing fine."

"That's good." He frowns.

I watch him go into the bedroom. He puts his arm around his girlfriend and comments to her about the people at the party. He's in control.

But an hour or so later, out on the back porch to get some air, I watch as he steps through the kitchen door and walks quickly to the railing and kneels. He vomits.

Emotion! Passion; excitement; nerves strung too high: how typical of the poets, I think, and how grand, this susceptibility to feeling in someone so charismatic!

Later that night, drunk, I watch Barry Edmonds—another charismatic poet, an older man, with a shaved head and eyes the same blue as faded denim—I watch as he ignores his wife, who earlier in the night has accused him of hitting her and now, snubbed by the poets, smiles at him, hunched over, wringing her hands, her face, made up with pink and red, smeared by tears so that her lips looked crayoned, their colour spreading to her chin and cheeks in a clown's grin.

That January Rufus returns. And one freezing day when Popeye and Gene aren't home he and Paul come over to check the house out.

While Paul and I watch, Rufus walks slowly through the hall. He stares at the photographs of the poets. We go downstairs. In front of a framed poem by John Newlove, Rufus stops. He reads it carefully. Then he turns and says, "This is good. This is quite good. And you're living with these guys."

"Yeah I am."

"That's great! Why didn't you *tell* us about this?"

He takes hold of my shoulders.

"You've been out of town. Jesus Christ."

"Well now I'm *back* in town."

"You want to meet them?"

"Of course I want to meet them."

"Okay then. They meet at the Egmont. On Thursday."

He looks sideways, as if noticing something. Then he glances at me. "Isn't that the place where your friend was drinking when…."

"That's the place."

"So you wanna go there?"

"Sure."

That Thursday an arctic front blows in. When I step off the bus downtown it's snowing. I head up an alley, walking in the falling snow past wooden crates and mounded-up piles of wet cardboard. Even in the cold the alley reeks. The street beyond is a relief. The streetlights hold up cones of whirling snow. I walk in the falling snow toward the pink and blue neon of the Egmont Hotel and push open the black door that Alistair first opened for me in 1970.

Beer smell. I hear my name and look around.

"Over here!"

Rufus and Paul and a young woman in a black cape are standing against the wall. Above them hangs a dim beer parlour lamp and a picture of a baseball team. The glass over the photo is so tarred with cigarette smoke you can hardly make out the faces. I know them all, though: I stared at the picture dozens of times in those days when Alistair and I and the rest of the Adanac gang spent our afternoons smoking up and our evenings getting drunk. Old times on Cordova Street. In summer the windows were dark with the leaves of trees, and wooden stairs down the back made a convenient place for people to sit and smoke hashish in the sun.

But now it's winter; and in the gloom it takes me a moment to see that the young woman is Ann Donet, the girl with the mild white face in our American Lit class. Rufus is touching her, laughing his manic laugh. He smiles; his eyes gleam. He's wearing a skull cap and has on a long khaki parka that comes to below his knees. The sleeves are so long I can only see his hands when he lifts them to light a cigarette.

Because of Ann's presence, Rufus's happiness, and the snow falling outside, the dark bar feels festive. Yet it hasn't lost its atmosphere. In the cone of light over the pool table two girls wearing jean jackets over unzipped kangaroo jackets eat pieces of garlic sausage and take turns shooting. One snaps her fingers when she sinks her ball. She turns and looks at us. She has a coarse face, a big nose, big breasts behind a tee shirt that says Slippery When Wet.

The poets are on the other side of the pool table, backed against a wall. In years to come I'll think sometimes of how exotic their clothes and faces looked; how solemn. They sit banded together like birds, whereas in the rest of the bar the happy passing back and forth of beers is starting which by the end of the night will end with one enormous table and with breeding taking place out in the parking lot.

"Come on, sit with us," Gene calls out.

We pull up a table and sit.

Richard walks over holding a tray heavy with glasses of beer.

"Fill up the table?" He makes a circling motion with his hand. Folded bills poke between the fingers of the other hand like the wads of cotton women place between their toes when they're painting their nails. When I say "Sure," he puts the beers down fast, their heads foaming over the waspwaisted glasses.

I hand him a five and a two. "Take one for yourself."

He nods.

I down my glass in a gulp and Gene nods and smiles. "That's the way. Hey Bruce, this is Bob. Bob, this is Bruce. Bob's just published a book."

Bob fills his chair from side to side. He has a bushman's beard. He looks like a logger in his black and red wool coat and high-topped boots

"Hey Bob," I say. "Congratulations."

"Woof," Rufus says. He lifts a leg.

"What's that smell?"

"What smell?"

And now everyone is leaning forward and talking.

"You Bob Rose?"

"No, that's another guy."

"Bob Rose aint no poet. He believes in ideas."

"Bad move."

"Hey Zonko!"

Billy Little has walked in with a woman who's wearing a miniskirt that gives her the blousy look of an old hooker. She has a dry sad face, eyes black with makeup. She points to the copies of *Ghost Horse* on the table. "I just finished reading it."

"Whaddya think?" Gene says.

"I love Artie's piece. It's so good."

"Yeah, I thought so. Yeah. "

I haven't seen this issue yet. I flip through it. But I'm too excited to read and already a little drunk. I hand it to Rufus. He reads steadily, moving from page to page. I wait, drinking, smoking, watching him.

Then he stops. "What is this?" he says. "This is pitiful. This is pitiful Black Mountain stuff."

I put my finger to my lips.

Ann says, "They can hear you."

"Good."

"It can't be all bad," Paul says.

"Show me a good one."

I pick up the magazine and leaf through it. "This one aint bad."

Rufus reads the poem. "Bruce, this is bad."

He again starts reading the magazine. He grins and mutters something in Ann's ear. As I stand up, Ann softly laughs.

In a dark corner by the washroom, a black man has his arm under the shirt of a blonde who sits on his knee. Her lips are dark with lipstick, her eyes drunk.

I piss standing at one of the old long urinals, near a window with a streetlight shining in. A winter night, the little room cold and smelling of shit, its acoustics echoey. I watch thick flakes of snow fall in the streetlight. "Falling snow," Alistair said, "the way it looks and smells. You can feel it in *Under the Volcano*. In those Mexican cantinas. That's why that's the greatest book ever written about Vancouver." I remember that now.

I step out of the washroom and watch a man stroke his cue. He sinks the ball. He bends over the felt and strokes again. The cue ball slips into a side pocket. At that moment the old feeling of sittig drunk in a bar imagining that at any second Cate will walk in overwhelms me. An extraordinary deja vu: I feel all the old pain; everything here, down to the sound of the cue ball sliding into the pocket, has happened before.

When I return to the table Rufus is slouched down in his chair. His legs are out and apart. One hand grips his glass of beer. I recognize this: it's his "fighting" pose. The rest of the group is staring at him.

"What's the circulation of your magazine?" Rufus is saying. "Who reads it outside your little circle?"

Barry Edmonds, sombre, pale-eyed, stares at him. "That little circle is the best writers in BC, asshole."

"The best writers? I'm talking about *read-ers. Read-ers.* People outside your fucking peer group."

He raises his beer and stares at Edmonds. He's slouched down so far in his seat the raised glass of beer is level with his head. "Do you understand what I'm saying? Or is it just too complicated for you? *Read-ers.*"

"Hey, we can hear you," Gene says.

"Good."

"What do you know about writing? You a writer?" Edmonds says.

"No. I don't need to be a writer, as you call it, to know you have problems."

"Problems. What an idiot." Edmonds lifts his glass and drinks.

"No, let him talk," the mini-skirted poet says.

"Come on, spill it," Popeye says. You got something to say, so say it."

They're all looking at him.

"So what's wrong with the magazine?" Gene says.

"It's simple. Your writing stinks of mimicry. You've got no conception of what your own poetry would even sound like. And you—" he lifts his chin at Bob in his wool coat and big beard who's grinning and shaking his head. "Who d'you think you are—Nature Boy?"

Bob stares at him. After a second he says, "What is with the insults, man?"

"I'm not insulting you. I'm asking a question."

"Okay, look." Bob's voice is trembling; it's odd to hear that tremble in such a big man. "I think the thing we do in situations like this is we step outside. Okay?"

"No. I'm not going to step outside That's for loggers. I'm not a logger, hunkered down in Williams Lake or wherever, running away from the world."

Edmonds stands up. He pushes Rufus in the chest. "Hey. Shut the fuck up."

"I won't shut up," Rufus says. "Not for a bunch of colonials—" but before he can say more Edmonds pulls him out of his chair and pushes him again in the chest so that he falls over.

Almost immediately Rufus stands up again, white-faced, his eyes black. He's still holding his glass. Just for a moment I see a look almost of pleading in his eyes. I look at Paul for help. He nods and says, "Look, we're sorry about this—" only to be cut off by Rufus.

"I'm not *sorry*," Rufus says, sitting back down. But when Ann takes his arm and starts to lift him he stands up, his face alarmed and sad-looking.

I put a hand on Rufus's other arm. "Come on, man, let's get out of here. Come on, Ann."

"Don't *worry*," Rufus says. "I'm *fine*."

But he isn't fine. His face remains white—he's shocked. We go out and slowly walk down the icy wooden stairs to the parking lot and Paul's old Barracuda. It's stopped snowing. The moon burns in the night sky. It shines like a spotlight on the new snow on the parking lot pavement. We slip and slide on the black ice and then get into Paul's car, whose heater doesn't work.

We drive down Hastings, all of us shivering and bent forward looking out the windows. Our breath appears and disappears. We're going to my place first.

After a while Paul breaks the silence. He smiles and looks into the rear view mirror. "You pissed them off."

"I did, I did." Rufus, sitting in the back, is hugging himself. Ann has her arm around him. "I know. Idiots. Doukhobours, that's what they are. Fundamentalists."

I say, "They couldn't take it."

"No, they couldn't."

I'm turned in the front seat looking at him and Ann. Rufus sits hunched forward. He looks out at the old houses going past, tall and dark in the winter night. Snow lies on their sheds and wooden staircases. "Fuck I hate this town," he says.

Three months later he'll leave for England. Two months after that Paul will leave, and I'll be on my own.

Alone. Did Alistair know this would happen? In later years I'll often think of something he said to me one evening when we were drunk but still able to talk to each other.

"Bruce," he said, "you and me, we have to go down. That's the only way for us. Our road is failure."

"Failure. It sounds bad," I said.

"It'll lead us to grace."

"It'll lead you to grace."

"You too. You too man."

It didn't lead me to grace. It led me to the post office.

Years after the old world disappeared that I knew with Alistair and Ray and that I saw for the last time in the Odlum Drive house, Colin Upton will tell me: "I want to produce a record of the Vancouver I know before it disappears forever." I'll understand that. I'll understand it because it will seem to me more and more that I went into the post office to make time stand still.

It's years ago now that I started there; but I just have to walk by the heavy Homer Street doors of the downtown plant and it all comes back as I first saw it, with the casuals streaming through the truck entrance into the basement and the building itself seeming like a physical emblem of the Vancouver that I'd returned to in 1970: the floors like airport hangers, the strips of overly intense fluorescent light, the TV cameras aimed at the workers, the way you'd sort or cull or throw, and each movement, each flick of the wrist and bending of the body, would repeat the previous movement until you were locked in a jelly of tedium. Once again I'm working graveyard; once again, already exhausted, though I've just started my eleven to seven shift, and having awoke only an hour ago from a dream in which Alistair is still alive and in which the intense white light, dirty floors, crowdedness and overwhelming noise have imprinted themselves, I walk across the floor and sit on my stool.

At this moment, blinking under the intense cold light, I feel degraded. Nothing around me is what I hoped for when I came back to the city. The harsh light, the unnatural hour, the supervisors watching the clerks, the rows of people all bent in front of their cases in exactly the same posture, the slack faces, the way somebody lets a letter slip from his hands and doesn't have the energy to bend down and pick it up: it all speaks of humiliation. I've never been in a place where there's such a sense of failure and a kind of soft, sagging hopelessness, a sense that's made even sharper by the rock music that comes out of the radio someone has on. It's music for people who dream their lives away, and it produces the same emotions in me that I know it produces in everyone else. Vague dreams, vague fantasies, that dull sweet feeling of heartache that a cheap late-night rock song can bring on— for minutes I exist in this mood, slumped over with a handful of mail in my left hand and a postcard in my right, staring at the image of Australia on the card in a kind of reverie. Then I think: This is how it happens, and I straighten my back, and then get right off my stool and sort standing up.

The post office will become my life, its walls familial, its people familial. In time I'll find in its unchanging environment a cure for the seasickness that constant change has induced in me. But not at first. At first, unable to get enough sleep, I feel an aimless bitterness when I'm away from work; and when I am at work I hate it. At six-thirty in the morning, with the shift nearly over, I watch the people around me move wearily, standing with a parcel in their hands, unable to think where it should go, staring at the address on a letter, and I think: What amount of money could be worth this?

One day in the Odlum Drive house, staring at the tattered map of BC that curled from the wall in Gene's bedroom, I saw with an almost hallucinatory clarity what Alistair had seen in old Vancouver with its dirty sidewalks littered with smashed whiskey bottles and soggy pieces of hot dogs. And I thought, looking at the map: No wonder he loved Ray so much. And no wonder Ray loved him.

A moment of understanding. But now in the post office that time of understanding seems like an interlude, no more.

An interlude. One morning many years later, coming home from work on the bus and thinking about that long-ago time when Alistair died, I have a moment when I feel the atmosphere of that period so strongly that just past Main I decide to get off. It's a windy Saturday morning, with white and grey clouds in the sky and crows flying under those clouds. I decide I'll walk through the Downtown Eastside.

It's been years since I've gone into that neighbourhood. I remember the people, still looking the way they did when Alistair drew them: the shy eyes, the smiles that show missing teeth. I remember how white the whiter clouds always seemed here, contrasting not only with the greyer parts of the sky, as they do in the rest of Vancouver, but with the buildings of rain-blackened wood.

The essential conservatism of East Vancouver grips me. And as the crows fly above the bus wires and I feel the cold wind on my face, I turn down Odlum toward the docks.

I can smell the ocean. I come up to the old wooden building where the whores lived; in a second, I think, I'll see the blackberry bushes where all those years ago condoms dangled from the thorns. And then the house....

But it's gone. With a kind of seamlessness, as if it never existed, a car lot stands at the corner where the house was. On the lot's roof a billboard advertises a Toyota truck. The car lot's sign is in Korean. Well-dressed Asian people walk around examining the cars. A few yards from me two men confer. The women they're with, both wearing puffy, ankle-length coats, also talk.

I watch the wives in their coats. And a strange thought occurs to me: they're standing in almost the exact spot where Brian Fawcett, tasting bile, knelt and stared out at the street. For minutes I gaze at the wives, seeing through them, as it were, to that night when we had the halloween party.

Then even the idea of the house fades. Around me instead is the common light of day.

II

5. The Spaceship

I

Tonight, an argument. Gunther has just said something that angers Bobby Gass, the oldest man in our entry group. Bobby's thin lips are pressed together. For a moment he glares at Gunther, who's sorting next to him; then he says: "You should be grateful you got a job."

"Nonsense," Gunther says. He rifles a letter hard into his case. As usual he's sitting with his back erect and with his shoes on the top rung of his stool so that his knees stand up nearly by his ears.

He wears pressed jeans; that and his harsh voice and the erect, monkeyish posture all give an impression of vitality and intelligence.

Gunther was my age, and like me he had recently left school. That drew us together. What kept us together was his humour. This humour made us friends; but it was also this humour that allowed me to see how much anger he carried around, how much fear and uncertainty about himself. He was a little bit wild, like a deer or a horse, and seeing that wildness in him I had gravitated toward him and tried to sort with him when I could.

Tonight we were working on the forward primary. The cases there were in rows, tall upright structures made of metal, with dozens of holdouts for the letters and a ledge in front on which the trays of mail were put. The tops of the cases had a thick fur of dust on them, so that if you put your bag or pack up there it came away grimy. So what you saw along the rows were bags or packs on the floor by each of the stools. I'd gotten so I could tell who was sitting where by looking for their pack; and tonight as usual I'd spotted Gunther's green one in the second row, near the end where our supervisor stood at a wooden desk that was like a lectern.

We were still "new"; so that was where we sat: there by Shirley Wong, asking her questions, sucking up to her in an attempt to establish ourselves. It was what all the "new" people did. You might have loathed the place and felt superior to everyone around you; but at least for the first few months you regressed to the position of a good little boy or girl, huddled together with all the other people in your entry group at the end where Shirley stood.

When Bobby got up from his stool to go to the washroom, I looked over at Gunther. "What were you and him arguing about?"

"The Spaceman. Donald. I told him I can't stand working with freaks."

"Well, here he comes now." I could see Donald at the end of the row.

"Excellent. The very best."

Donald slowly came toward us, talking loudly as he walked. He was wearing a tight scarlet jumpsuit that was unzipped to show the hairs on his chest turning into a bush around his belly button. Combined with his badly-shaven face and dull eyes that didn't look at the person he was talking to, that flash of nakedness gave him the soiled appearance of a catamite.

He stopped beside Ruth Price, who was sorting on the other side of me. Ruth wore jeans that stretched in tight lateral creases across her heavy hips. Eyeing those hips, and standing so close that his shoulder touched hers, Donald reached over and put a hand on her vulva.

Ruth said, "Donald, you got to stop that." She calmly removed his hand.

"I like you."

"I know you do. But you can't just touch me like that."

"You got me excited."

"I can see that."

"I want to jack off." He tittered.

"Well, you can't jack off in public, Donald. Maybe you should go up to the can."

Gunther slammed in a letter. "If he comes near me, I'll rip his nose out with my thumbs."

Tough talk; but I knew it meant nothing. Up in the wash-room ten minutes later, standing beside me, Gunther watched in silence as two bulky mailhandlers reached up and took beers from the dozen or so that were kept in the water tank above the urinal. As they drank, a friend of theirs walked up the steps. In a voice as hard and emphatic as a rifle shot, one of the drinkers shouted, "Hey, you fucking maggot, how's it going!" and I saw Gunther's face tighten with fright.

I thought: Why is he here? I didn't know. But he didn't belong. He had had a difficult upbringing—an only child in an upper-middle-class home with remote parents, bullying in high school, and then residence in a student dormitory at UBC—and now all around him were the jeans and pot bellies of the working class. We worked with people who couldn't live without drugs, who drank on the job, who listened incessantly to rock and roll, and whose intelligence and animal spirits had in many cases been corrupted by years of working in the plant, a corruption you could trace in the ugly graffiti that filled the walls of the freight elevators. It all offended Gunther; and when we got back from the washroom (and with Ruth looking at him in a way that combined amusement and discomfort), he joked about the clerks sorting around us with a vehemence that made me snigger. For the next half hour we covered them all: the mentally disturbed coder who always bought two pieces of pie on his coffee break and gobbled them up with a disgusting quickness, the speechless women whose eyes slid away whenever you looked at them, the crazies like Rachel who wore a wig made of cloth strands under a hard-hat and a sign on her back that said "Rachel for Jesus," the eccentrics who talked to themselves, the ones who smelled. And the union bulletins with their strident anger, the shop stewards who trotted around nagging us clerks and not doing any work—that too we laughed at.

Finally Ruth turned to Gunther. "I notice," she said, "that you don't put Shirley down."

"What d'you mean, Shirley?"

"Shirley Wong. Our supervisor." She pointed.

"But why should I put her down, as you say?"

"You tell me."

Gunther stared at her. "You mean because she wears a skirt? Because she has authority? Somebody needs to have authority in this place."

Ruth shrugged.

That night our group was called together to meet with a steward up on the sixth floor, and Shirley came up with us. The steward tried to get her to leave the room, his voice flustered and nervous.

"What an idiot," Gunther muttered.

I nodded.

The steward insisted. He paced back and forth, a little man

with his jeans pulled up to his waist, anxiously twiddling the fingers of one hand so fast they blurred. "Shirley," he said, "you know that according to the contract the Union has the right to speak to new employees alone for fifteen minutes."

Gunther said, "And what do you need that right for?"

I smiled. But the steward ignored the comment and continued to press Shirley to leave. Finally she did; and for the next ten minutes, after handing out contracts that were left behind by half the people in the room, the steward faced a barrage of questions.

Geraldine said: "Why did Shirley have to leave?"

Bobby said: "Why does the union put out those bloody bulletins? They're just propaganda."

The steward said, "They're not propaganda—" and I interrupted him: "You could be a little more civil, you know."

Later, back in the hallway with Gunther, I flipped my contract up into the air.

"Mao's little blue book," I said.

Spring. Smells in the wet air, the scent of new growth making its way even through the open windows of the fourth floor washroom.

Quiet all up and down the rows tonight.

I walked down the washroom steps, walked across the floor and climbed onto my stool. I looked at my watch. 2:10. The last time I'd looked it had said 1:43. I looked at Gunther. He's half asleep, his eyes lidded, hunched over as he sorts.

Deeply bored, I climb down from my stool. I crook an orange plastic tray in my arm and start walking up my row pulling out the Thunder Bay mail.

As I walk, I feel what I always do when I'm pulling mail: as if I'm the Invisible Man, standing right beside people and sometimes even touching their shoulders, but still totally ignored.

And then something happens that changes my life in the

plant.

It starts when I reach Smoky. He's a gaunt, hunched-over man who always sorts alone and who's gotten his nickname because he has to go to the washroom every twenty minutes to have a cigarette. He talks to no one. His only stimuli are the different stamps and the handwriting on letters; and so he sorts with amazing slowness, staring at each letter until he's sucked out every bit of visual nourishment that the piece of mail offers.

Smoky rarely clears out his case. And tonight every holdout is jammed with mail. In his Toronto and Kitchener-Waterloo holdouts the mail hangs out into the air like an upside-down ski jump. I stand beside him and fill half a tray from his Thunder Bay holdout, studying him as he works.

A complex emotion takes hold of me.

Smoky's fingers are painted with tobacco tar. The insides of his middle and index fingers are a deep brown, almost black. But the fingers are long, and Smoky's face, the cheeks caved in, the eyes wet, looks elegant, in a manner painted by El Greco.

But I most admire his long, horny, clawlike fingernails. Discoloured also, they've twisted and curled; yet they're cut straight across, and they give me an impression of a life both miserable and touched by piety.

Made reflective and tender by this new mood, I pass old Ethel, a middle-aged man named Jerry, a sad fat boy named Al who wears a heavy black digital watch strapped tightly to his wrist. Loners. But most of the people I walk past sort in groups of two or three. When they take their "can breaks"—a plant institution: everyone takes washroom breaks, and most people take them at a regular time, usually once an hour—they put a small handful of mail on their stool, thereby marking it as theirs.

This is important. To be able to sit with a friend, to be able to have a friend to talk to, makes life easier; and anyone who tries to take someone's stool is immediately put in their place. So like

Gunther and me, people have gotten in the habit of sitting in particular spots in order to be able to talk to each other; and as I walk up and down the rows, picking up my mail, I listen to their conversations.

It's very quiet. I hear no laughter, none of the vivacity you'd find in the daytime. People are too tired for that. Their murmuring voices, they way they half-turn their heads to each other, their pauses and occasional sighs, and along with that, the rumbling sound of the big belts going overhead that you can only hear late at night when the machines are off—all this contributes to the sense I have tonight of being in a spaceship far away from the rest of society.

And then it happens, the completion of the process that started while I was pulling Smoky's mail. Suddenly, in the middle of the third row, happiness fills me, a joy so great that I tremble. People have surrendered to their fates. They aren't competing with each other. Their conversations are as simple and trivial as the murmuring of two people in bed. I can sense the exhaustion behind it all, and the basic animal sadness, but I've come from a world where you never stop competing, and the sheer humility of the people I'm walking among overwhelms me. So much so that for the next few nights I just have to shut my eyes as I work for the happiness to return.

But there's another side to the coin. That Sunday night Gunther and I and Jules Marchand, a small man with a pot belly who's a couple of years older than us, start our shift on the opening table. It's simple work; but it uses the muscles, and because it's Sunday Jules has brought a radio to work along with his usual thermos of coffee and vodka.

"Okay, it's midnight," Gunther says, looking at his watch. "Time for Katy."

"Excellent," Jules says, and changes the dial on the radio.

Katy Malloch opens with Oliver Nelson's "Stolen Moments." Jules turns it up. The music—majestic, full of emotion—pours forth, and for the next few minutes we work in a state of exaltation. When the song ends, Gunther climbs up onto the table to open the bags; I start lobbing parcels backwards over my shoulder into the coffins; and Jules, drinking in swift gulps from his thermos, says: "I'm telling you for a fact. Willy's cat talks to him."

"Will's a fucking dink," Gunther says, "bringing an animal into the plant."

"Anyway, cats can't talk," I say.

"They can."

"No they can't."

"I heard him," Jules says. "He said, 'Willy doesn't treat me right.'"

I laugh. I turn, lobbing a parcel; and as I turn, a supervisor named Debra Porter walks up, dressed in shiny high-heeled shoes, a tight dark skirt against which her thighs press, a black shirt with the sleeves turned up once and the two top buttons undone. She smiles at me; then she stands right behind Jules, maybe a foot from his back, and, still smiling, taps him on the shoulder.

"I'd like you to turn the radio off, Jules."

I notice that Jules's jeans are baggy. His shoulders slump. His hands grab the edge of the table. He sighs.

Debra shifts slightly. Now she stands so close to Jules it's as if she's flirting with him.

"One more time, Jules. Turn the radio off."

Jules's face has become blotched, the dermis under the skin suffused in big patches with blood. I see that his eyes are squeezed shut and shame fills me.

"Turn it *off*, Jules."

"All right."

Jules ungrips the table, and with his head down and his cheeks and forehead mottled with the red blotches, he walks over to the radio and turns it off.

Up in the washroom later, standing side by side, we lean over the wide windowsill and look out at the empty car park across Homer Street. I say, "You should just ignore the bitch."

"I don't want to ignore her. I want to bust her ass."

"Well? Then do it."

No response.

I try again. "You know what Debra is. She's a bully. She's just like all the other bullies in this hole."

Jules sighs. Then he starts to shiver. His whole body is trembling. "I used to have a girlfriend in Calgary who would say things like that. 'Ignore them. Ignore them.' Sure. How can you ignore somebody when they fucking frighten you. Because that's what happens. I see her coming and I freeze. Isn't that great?" Jules is trembling so hard he has his arms around himself.

II

By three a.m.—lunchtime—tiredness lay on people's faces. It lay on their clothes, the piles of canvas bags, even the rows of metal cages lined up on the third floor. But in the brightly lit cafeteria it swarmed on the surfaces of things like an hallucination.

The cafeteria was on the top floor. It was a large room with floor-to-ceiling windows that at night had orange curtains pulled across them. It contained about twenty round white tables, and I always thought it would have been fine if it was clean. But it rarely was: usually trash lay everywhere and you had to watch where you sat—coffee or juice might have been slopped onto the floor.

Tonight french fries littered the floor, ketchup stains covered the tables as well as coffee puddles absorbed by drenched brown napkins; and on almost every table sat ripped-apart styrofoam cups with holes burnt into them that had been used as ashtrays. Because of the intense light everything hit me in the eyes, and the first thing I did when I sat down with my lunch was obsessively wipe off the table.

But as always what most unsettled me entering the cafeteria was the sadness in people's faces, the almost frightening lack of affect. Nowhere did I see or hear any of the cheerful buzz and wandering around from group to group that you'd expect in a company cafeteria. Instead there was atomization. People sat here and there, gobbling food or reading or just trying to sleep with their heads on their arms.

At first glance everyone seemed to be alone. Only recently had I noticed that small groups of people regularly sat at the same tables. And even now, knowing this, I was unwilling to join Ruth and Bobby and Geraldine and Col Grendel who were waving me over. It was just too difficult. The ugliness of the room, my shyness, my extreme tiredness, the fact that Gunther, after a few bad fights with me, had moved to a ten p.m. start time and so wasn't there to help me break the ice —all this kept me sitting at my table alone, pretending not to see Ruth's raised hand, sitting so rigidly that the muscles in the back of my neck tightened.

Then Geraldine called out: "Bruce, come on over!"

I couldn't ignore this. I put my Denver sandwich back on my tray; and I walked over and sat down.

Immediately I regretted it. The conversation was constrained, and again and again silence came over everyone. After one such silence Bobby said, "It's a long night eh?"

Ruth said, "It's a long night."

And suddenly there was nothing to say—and the five of us stared at the table top, one tearing a match apart, another ripping a styrofoam cup into shreds, unable all the time to raise our eyes and look at each other.

The next minute was a little agony. But then I saw Gunther, who had slipped away from the floor to get some chocolate milk. He raised a hand, signalling me.

"Excuse me," I said to the group. "I got to go talk to that guy."

When I sat down with him, Gunther said, "I'm quitting. I decided tonight."

I took a bite out of my sandwich and looked into space. "Probably a good idea." Already I felt distant from him.

Gunther said, "How's the night proceeding?"

I told him about the silence at the other table.

He said, "I hate it when that happens." He looked at me. "So why are you staying in this hole?"

"I don't know."

"That's no answer."

"No, it's not."

"So why are you staying."

The anger that had already come between us flared in me. "I don't know. Okay?"

And I didn't. But I did stay. And as the months passed and fall gave way to winter, my relationship to the people around me changed. I learned people's names; I became friends with some of them. Adopting the style of the plant, I started to wear a work apron and sometimes even a tee shirt, though its tightness and the air on my bare arms made me feel exposed and vulnerable. And each night, as I waited for the freight elevator to unload, or sorted letters, or threw parcels—standing at times in one spot with the patience of an animal—I felt the rhythm of my new life take hold of me, a rhythm that began when I awoke in the dark and ended when I rode home on the bus in the first light of day, exhausted, my face and body slack, feeling only a blank melancholy and the voluptuous desire for sleep.

The biggest of those social groups that gathered in the cafeteria— I always thought of it as the Head Table—centred around an enormously fat, red-faced man named Dick. One night in February I was sitting across from him when the topic of Harold came up.

Geraldine Tremblay started it. It was she who had invited me to sit with the group a few months earlier, and it was she who kept the conversation alive when it seemed to be dying. I liked Geraldine; I liked her chattiness, her warm heart, and the way she always walked with her breasts and head held high, as if she was marching up to receive a medal. She talked with tremendous gusto; and now she turned this gusto to Dick, leaning across to him and touching his shoulder.

"So you're going to Surface next week, Dickie."

Dick nodded.

"You're gonna have to work with Harold, you know."

"No. You got that wrong. Harold's gonna have to work with me."

Laughter all around. And suddenly everyone was talking.

"God, that Harold is so fucking crazy."

"He stinks."

"You know how he writes the tags a certain way? Man, if you try to write them different, he's just on you. It's like he's the boss there."

"That's the problem," Dick said. "He's never been rotated out of Surface. He thinks he owns the place. And he thinks he can keep me outa there. Well, he can't."

Dick leaned back and, the king of the table, immense, his belly in his tee shirt hanging down between his legs over his genitals, he applied chapstick to his lips. He mashed his purplish lips together like a woman with her lipstick. "I don't mind him, you know. I seen worse. Harold is Harold."

Now I joined in. "He hates you."

Dick looked at me.

"I'm on Surface right now and Harold and I talk. He calls you 'the pig.'"

"Yeah? What do you say?"

"I tell him you're okay."

More laughter.

Lunch over, I took the escalators down to the third floor and walked over to Surface Despatch. Harold looked up from the book he was reading, a startling figure, tall and white-faced, strands of greasy hair on his bony cheeks, his pale eyes staring and inquisitive.

"You have a good lunch?"

"Uh huh. What about you?"

But he didn't answer. He had turned his back to me and was

already working.

I started dropping parcels into one of the racked string bags.

"No. That's wrong. That's wrong," Harold said. He grabbed the parcel from my hand. "That size parcel goes *here.*" He dropped the parcel into the bag next to the one I had dropped it into.

"Why does it go there?" I said.

He stared at me, then turned away.

I walked over to him and looked at him. "Why does it go there?"

His eyes turned away and he kept working.

I touched his arm. "Why does it go there?"

"Don't touch me! It goes there because I say so!"

"That's ridiculous. There's no distinction between those bags."

"Listen to me. I make the rules here. And this is the way it is." He was enraged; his rage had hardened his voice.

I stared at him: a man in his early thirties, tall and skeletal, with straight black hair down to the middle of his back, wearing a tee shirt and jeans that were filthy with ground-in dirt.

"You're mad," I said.

He smiled, as if he had won a point. "That may be."

A few nights later Harold was once more being talked about in the cafeteria. Dick was going to Surface after lunch, and people were speculative.

"He looks like Dracula," said Geraldine, who was sitting next to me. "Watch he doesn't bite you, Dick."

"I like that," Col said. "Dracula. Yeah. Like he was born here. Like maybe he rose up one night out of a pile of string bags and there he is."

"Yep. Sun comes up he folds himself into a locker," Dick said.

There was silence for a moment.

"I can't stand his stink," Col said.

Dick nodded. His small bear's eyes stared at us all. "You know what he smells like?" he said. "He smells like a ferret."

"You know who smells worse?" Col said.

"Who."

"The Bobbsey Twins."

I said, "Who're they?"

"Over there." Dick pointed to two women standing in line at the counter whose bums and hips were so enormous they were like tires of fat that moved independently of the rest of their bodies.

"They stink of shit cause they can't wipe themselves," Col said.

'That's awful," Geraldine said.

"The twins aren't the worst," Col said. "You know Denise, that part-timer with the red hair? She fucks men in the basement, and I hear she sells her panties to guys cause of the shit stripes."

"Ha ha ha ha ha!" Geraldine's face had turned red with joy. "No! No!"

"I swear to fucking god."

"Her ass is okay but she needs to have her cunt cleaned." Dick stuck out a long red tongue.

"Ha ha ha!" Geraldine shrieked. "Stop! Stop! I'm gonna piss myself I'm laughing so hard!"

Lunch ended. Dick and I and a woman we called Little Toni headed down the escalator to the third floor.

In her calm way Little Toni said, "What do you think he'll do?"

Dick shrugged his fat shoulders.

Walking across the floor toward Surface we saw Harold—who always ate his lunch there—stand up looking tall and alarming with his waist-length black hair. He did in fact look like a

165

vampire. He started walking toward Dick, waving his hands in the air, gesturing him back, and telling him he couldn't work there.

"Fuck that," Dick said. He walked toward Harold with a fat man's straight-backed waddle. His face was red, but he had his arms at his sides.

He moved toward the bag racks. Harold stepped in front of him.

Harold said, "Get out of here."

Dick said, "Look. Just get out of my way."

Instead Harold stepped forward and kicked him, a hard kick just above the knee with his boot. Dick put his arms up in the traditional boxer's stance and punched Harold in the stomach. But Harold hardly noticed. He kicked Dick again with his boot, then kicked him again, and then again.

Within moments Dick's face had turned reddish-purple. He was gasping so hard he seemed to be shuddering. He stepped forward with his breath whistling and his fat arms held up; but as soon as he got in close Harold reached over and ripped hanks of his long, thinning, white-blonde hair off his head, kicking him all the while with his heavy boot.

In seconds hair lay all over the floor. Later somebody gathered it up and gave it to Dick.

The fight ended quickly—the two men were pulled apart by supervisors. But the violence of the fight stayed in the air. And as I got to work I kept trying to assimilate the ugly thing that had happened. I didn't want to touch the hair on the floor. But again and again I caught myself looking at it. That was Dick's hair; it had been ripped off his head. How painful it must have been! And the kicking, and the shuddering breath, and the sense of things out of control! it was the anarchy of the situation that finally began to seen the most dreadful thing about it—the sense that there was no order anywhere and that at the merest impulse one man could start kicking violently at another.

I went about my work, throwing parcels into a row of iron cages. And gradually an almost panicky feeling of dismay took hold of me.

In the past months, I realized, I had started to sentimentalize the situation I was in. I had accepted it, even romanticized it; and in the process I had given up more and more of who I was in order to gain a secure identity. It was so simple: I wasn't Bruce Serafin anymore, someone outside of things and deeply unsure about his life. Instead I was a postie; the other workers were fellow-posties. And at certain moments when we were laughing or talking together, a kind of golden light of solidarity would descend, and my entire struggle with the question of how to live would just disappear.

But now with the fight this feeling of certainty had vanished. Anxiety grew in me. I felt separate from everything around me, with all sense of comradeship gone. I seemed to be face-to-face with myself.

I thought: We're all like animals. And then: You're nothing but a postie, you're nothing but a postie—over and over again.

My anxiety grew alarming. And finally I couldn't work anymore. I stopped, stared at the cages lined up in front of me, then turned and walked quickly toward the washroom, thinking furiously as I walked. I wanted to be alone and figure out what I was going to do.

Up in the washroom a few people nodded or raised a hand. To avoid them I went over to a window and looked out into the night, smoking steadily. I don't know how long I stood there—maybe twenty minutes. But after a long while the anxiety began to be replaced by sadness.

It was a relief, this sadness. It comforted me. I sighed; and that sigh, that slow, luxurious wallowing in my unhappiness, revealed to me all at once how it would be possible to spend a life in this place. The security, the sure feeling about yourself, would help; but finally it would be fatalism—a deep sense of resignation—that kept you there.

I leaned forward on the window sill. The fight, the desperation I felt after, then the comforting sadness, had all led to an insight: at the age of twenty-six I knew what it would be like to be a man of fifty wearing a postal apron.

6. Love and Death

I

When I started graveyard, I'd been a long time without a girlfriend; and early in my second year I fell in love. One night, standing on the steps leading to the washroom, rejected by Milena and trying to keep my eyes bright so as not to show my misery, I looked out over the fourth floor. I was high up; I could see and hear everything. I looked at the shiny concrete floor littered with pieces of strapping, the floor-to-ceiling pillars. the roaring Toshibas, the OCRs, the cages, the rows of people at the opening table and the people pushing binnies—and I thought: I'll never be able to leave. It was as if the plant and my infatuation with Milena were the same thing, as though if I left the plant, the love that gave my life meaning would die.

And I wasn't alone. Standing on the steps I could see Geraldine with her feather earrings and her skintight jeans slowly saunter past Billy the mailhandler, eyeing him with eyes that were sad and intent; I could see Will the bagboy standing at the end of the fourth row watching Paula Green sort, and I could see Jules Marchand, his gaze attached to her by an invisible thread, study Deb Angus as she slipped off her stool and headed toward the coat rack to get something from her coat. It was as if in a grotesque way the plant was made for love, as if the tiredness that lay on everything, the noise, the flourescent lights and even the piles of dirty canvas bags on the floor only sharpened the allure of the human beings who worked in the plant.

I descended the steps and walked across the concrete floor. Because Milena was sorting in the second row a heat of significance seemed to emanate from it. I entered the row and walked past her, not looking at her, yet feeling her presence brush against my side.

I got on my stool and started to sort. A half hour later, I heard her voice. "You want company?"

"Sure." Only after I'd spoken did I trust myself to look at her.

"I've been mean."

"It's okay."

We started to talk about the Chinese workers in the plant.

"They're different than us, you know."

Milena looked at me and shook her head. "What d'you mean, different."

"Well, they're different culturally. They don't think the way we do."

"God, that's such crap. Bruce, look around. I can tell you, I've been here eight years and they're no different than you and me."

"Okay."

We sorted.

"Where'd you get this idea that they're different?"

I tried to be light. "Well, let's see. Fu Manchu books. *Terry and the Pirates.*"

"*Terry and the Pirates*?"

170

"It's a comic strip."
"Oh, of course."

I didn't tell her that I had another and maybe more defensible reason for feeling disconcerted by the Chinese in the plant. Many of the clerks were Hong Kong expatriates; but in all my years in Vancouver the only Chinese I'd interacted with had been the East Vancouver and downtown Eastside Chinese who'd been around long before the big emigrations from Hong Kong. They managed grocery stores and bacon and egg cafes; and after decades of being tormented by the larger society they tended to be private people, full of their own concerns.

When I thought of them, simple images came to mind. I thought of their hard work; the shyness or wariness of the men; the raw harsh voices of the women; the plain clothes—sports-coats, black slippers; the children doing their homework under a lamp at the counter between ringing in orders of toast and scrambled eggs. And often the Chinese lived in the building in which they worked—upstairs or behind a curtained doorway in a room in which you would sometimes catch a glimpse of a TV set, a bird in a cage, or else a calendar with a picture of a white-cheeked Peking opera singer on it, eyes shadowed with red.

But now in the post office these familiar images fell apart. One hot summer night while I was working on a Toshiba I watched and listened as a young Chinese woman named Lucy Goon working one machine over four or five times asked Larry the supervisor for permission to go to the washroom.

Finally she hollered, "I need to pee!"
"Stay at your machine," Larry said.
"I really need to go!"
"No no no no no. Keep working."
"Larry, god damn it, I have to pee!"
"No. Stay at your job!"

Lucy stared at him. And then occurred one of those dream-like scenes that in later years would summon up for me the way the plant debased and made vivid the people who worked there. Lucy said, "Okay, you asked for it!" And she squatted by the Toshiba, pulled her pants down and, with her sweater held modestly over her lap (though I could see her pale thighs), pissed on the floor.

I stopped working. I laughed and clapped my hands. A few clerks in the front of the first two rows saw what was going on. They clapped and got off their stools. Then clerks all through the forward primary started coming out into the aisle, until Lucy and Larry were ringed by a crowd of people.

When Larry complained to the superintendent and Lucy's side of the story came out, Larry was told to clean the piss up himself. Not long afterward I realized that the Chinese, both in the plant and out on the street, no longer looked alike.

That fall we went on strike. I was asked to become a picket captain; and I accepted, because as a captain I would be allowed to walk the picket line from four p.m. to midnight instead of midnight to eight in the morning. But it was hard. Because you did nothing but walk or stand, you noticed the temperature: the heat in the late afternoon, the intense cold at night. By nine p.m. unemployed men came in off the street, wanting to join the line, and you had to talk to them—some were mentally ill. On the other hand, posties you'd been certain would show up didn't come to the line at all or else took their vacation leave.

Emotions raged. One night Coleen Brown, a shop steward who contained in her small body, like a pilot light in a stove, a continual tremble of anger, walked up to a supervisor standing in the middle of a truck entrance. She stopped under a streetlight whose hard light blanched her skin, and in a voice shrill and trembling with bravado, she shouted: "Hey Jack, why don't you come over and punch me out? I know you'd like to. Why don't you come and kick my face in? Actually, Jack, why don't you kiss my ass?" And with that she turned and pulled her pants down and mooned him, her naked rear end a vision under the streetlight's glare. The activists watching—Milena among them—screamed with delight.

The strike exhausted me. Milena had started wearing the leather jacket of a truck driver I'd recently seen her with; and each time I encountered her without being prepared for it, coming around a corner of the plant, say, my stomach tightened with grief.

One evening I saw the two of them leaning together against the plant wall. He was standing close to her with one hand on the wall. And seeing that hand so close that his little finger touched her rump—a rump I'd seen naked a dozen times in the past months, fleshy white hips and buttocks and thighs raised in the air so that her cunt and the eye of her anus were displayed to me, a vision that because of my youth I'd found nearly overwhelming—seeing this physical contact between them I felt a stab of unhappiness so intense I was unable to keep my face from expressing the anguish I felt.

I walked quickly up, as full of knowledge of what was to come as an old man. Heart hammering, I said, "I want to talk to you, okay?"

"I can't talk right now."

The driver—tall, mild-featured—looked at me.

Ignoring him, I said, "Are you going out with him?"

"What?"

"Are you seeing him?"

She looked at me angrily. "That's none of your business! I don't want to talk to you, okay? Just leave me alone. Find something else to do."

Find something else to do. Until I heard these words I had

felt old. Now I became callow, my misery stamped on my face.

When I went home that night, walking around downtown for a bit before catching the bus, I experienced something that went back to when we had first moved from Hinton: it was as if everything in front of me was taking place behind a sheet of glass.

It was all unexpected. But what most surprised me was the behavior of the coders from afternoon shift.

Canada Post had been one of the first big government organizations to hire Chinese Canadians. And by the time I entered the post office, entire families of Chinese descent worked there—two and sometimes three generations of them. In particular they worked as coders, a job I found almost unbearably tedious. When I started my shift I'd empty letters into a binny and watch them sitting at their group desk suites in long lines, one arm in their lap, the fingers of the other hand convulsing in quarter-second intervals. And I'd think: They're cooperative. They hang out together and go along with the way things are. I noticed that they only rarely got involved in union politics, and like many others I thought of them as passive and apolitical. I was wrong.

On the fourth night of the strike I was told that scabs were going to be picked up at a lot near Main and Seventh and bussed into the plant. The union secretary who told me this placed a pile of leaflets at my feet. "I was wondering if you could take these out there and distribute them," he said.

"I don't have a car," I said.

He nodded. Then he looked at me, his eyes mild. "You'll figure it out. I've got confidence in you." And with that I was caught.

But for the moment I couldn't do anything with them. I was arguing with Dave Thibaud, a CUPW militant whom I loathed for the way he'd jump to his feet at union meetings and with his mustache wet with spittle scream that we needed to shut the plant down.

Now he was yelling—not exactly at me, more at the night air. "Fuck these bullshit pamphlets! Those fucking scabs need to be smashed!"

The people of our section of the line—mostly coders —were staring at him. He was wild with excitement. He looked around and then he raised a fist in the air. "The people! United! Shall never be defeated!"

"Jesus, Thibaud. Shut up."

A half dozen teamsters who'd come by to join the line heard us. One of them walked over. He picked up a pamphlet and looked at it. He had huge hands, the fingers so thick they looked as if they'd been stung by bees.

"Whose idea is this?"

"It's our idea."

He looked at me. "This is nuts. You don't hand out pamphlets to scabs. This dude is right. You hammer them."

"No sir. No way. Our job is to hand these out. We don't hammer anybody." I was shaking my head and looking at him.

He looked right back. His eyes were steady. "I preciate what you're saying, man. But we're here to help you, man. You got to put the fear of God into those fuckers."

And with that he turned and said, "Come on, guys, let's go— Main and Seventh!" and the half dozen teamsters took off for their cars.

It was unbelievable. *Where was the union?* The teamster had seemed calm; but with his buddies he was also dangerous and out of control. And nobody was doing anything about it. I was too worried even to feel angry. I imagined big, thirty-dollar-an-hour men beating up skinny forty-year-olds and teenagers from Princess Street and Clark Drive.

I shivered and moved closer to the fire barrel. I tried to think of what to do. Two men walked over. One of them rubbed his hands together over the fire. I knew who he was: a kind of unofficial leader of the coders, a short, handsome man with a soft nose and a lock of dark hair falling over his forehead who often acted as a go-between, smoothing things out on the floor.

He said, "I overheard you and that guy. We got a problem."

"You're telling me."

He held out his hand and we shook.

"My name is Sun King."

"I'm Bruce."

He smiled at me. "Tell me how we can help."

And it was as if the words were a switch. It thrilled me to hear them. All at once it seemed action was possible. I started to think fast.

"We need a car."

The other man said, "I got a car. We can use it."

I knew him slightly. Up in the fourth floor washroom once he had asked me if I was a shop steward; when I'd said I wasn't, he had nervously laughed. His name was Steven Chou. He was young, with small eyes and hair that stuck up at the back of his head. His laugh had been quick and jerky, and with the casual racism I had then, I'd thought of it as Chinese nerves.

But now I saw his excitement differently. I saw that it was held in by his reserve. It was like a passion. It dignified and exalted him.

We smiled at each other, trying to make our smiles express everything we felt. "This is really good," I said. "Okay. Let's go. We got to get those guys!"

I grabbed the pamphlets and the three of us climbed into Steven's car and headed off. As we drove through the night excitement spurted in us. We alternately grinned and frowned, hardly able to talk.

When we got to the staging area where the scabs were being loaded onto the buses we saw maybe sixty or so people milling around in the dark. A wind had blown up and the shadows of tree branches whipped wildly in the street lights. Teamsters were pacing back and forth under the lights on the edge of the lot. Their shadows advanced toward the scabs and then retreated.

One of the teamsters shouted: "Go back into your holes! Get the fuck out of here!"

A skinny teenaged boy walked up to him. His face was defiant. "*You* get out of here!"

"What? Fuck off you punk!" The teamster, twice the kid's size, pushed him hard in the chest. The kid nearly fell. He backed off slowly, still staring at the teamster though even from where we stood we could see the fear in his face. The teamster stepped forward and again pushed the kid, hard.

"Fucking bastard," I said.

Sun King placed his hand on my arm. "Go easy."

We jumped out of the car. I ran ahead and put my hands on the shoulders of the teamster who had pushed the kid. Sun King stepped in front of him. "Enough of this!" he said. His voice was controlled. "You guys are not posties! This is not your business! Let's go now!"

The teamster stared at him. I thought something would happen. Sun King stood calmly, facing the big man. Then the teamster shook his head and turned away. The other teamsters stopped what they were doing. Within minutes they had gone back to their cars.

So easy it had been, in the end. But we weren't done. Upset by the teamsters, all the scabs had pulled together into a mass by the buses. They stood there in the dark watching us.

I said, "Someone's got to take these pamphlets and distribute them."

They glanced at me.

"I know I should do it," I said. "I'm just too timid to walk over there."

"I'll do it," Sun King said.

I looked at him with relief and gratitude. He smiled at me. "It's nothing."

Sun King took the pamphlets, left the car, and walked quickly across the parking lot to where the scabs were waiting. The kid who had stepped forward raised his fist. Sun King stopped. He talked to the boy slowly and softly, and the fist came down. Then Sun King stepped into the crowd, and all around him people were taking the pamphlets and looking at him, and soon people were asking him questions, and then he was so surrounded by people I couldn't see him anymore.

Later that night we all stood by the garbage can fire drinking Cokes. The night sky was clear and cold. The moon, like a giant stadium light, had just risen over the north shore mountains. Some of the female coders, their faces painted by the flames as if with iodine, started singing a Cantonese song that wavered in the air.

I saw Milena walking down the sidewalk. For the first time since the beginning of the strike I looked at her almost without grief. I still yearned for her; but I felt—after the night's achievement—a sense of calm; and this feeling of calm allowed me a detachment I hadn't had before.

But where was Sun King? Five minutes later I saw him. He strolled toward me, his ON STRIKE picket sign on his chest. To pass the time, he'd been walking around the plant. We smiled at each other; and again I thought how inadequate a smile was to express what I felt. As he walked by, one of the ladies pulled at his arm and gave him a Coke.

She had seen us smile. She caught my eye. "That's Sun King," she said. Then quickly, softly, laughing, made nearly breathless by her joke, she added, "He's our sun king!"

II

I'm sorting with two new friends, Sharon and Roland. Sharon is sorting between us. Roland says: "I couldn't take my eyes off Alice at the union meeting. She had piss stains on her pants. It was like she flooded herself."

"Oh I know, it was awful," Sharon says.

"You see the way she kept putting her hand down there? She kept rubbing her cunt with her fingers. And then she'd bring them up to her nose and sniff them."

"I saw her picking her nose."

"She was rooting in there. Hoeing. I thought she was trying to find her lucky penny."

Sharon laughs, a soft giggling laugh. She sorts; then says: "Andy was showing his cock."

"Not again."

"Oh yeah, he was sitting next to me. He had on those high-cut red shorts? He had one foot up. You could see right up there."

"Funny. He always says his cock is so ugly."

"Is it?"

"I don't think so."

"You've seen it?" I say.

"I've had it up my ass." Roland's hand flies to his mouth. "Oh, I'm sorry! Did I *offend* you?"

I'm with Sharon at a party on Graveley Street, just off Commercial Drive. It's summertime. We're sitting in the backyard. The sky is a burnt blue; the mountains are black cutouts. The lines of pea poles facing the alley at the edge of the small yard have begun to blur into the dark. On the other side of the high fence we can hear Chinese voices. "Real East Vancouver here," Sharon murmurs.

Many union activists are at this party, drinking and talking. With Sharon's help—she's a shop steward —I've started to know them. At the same time I have a growing sense that I'll never be considered trustworthy. I've moved and moved; I'm the product of a secular, middle-class culture. My dad's shyness and intellectual independence have ingrained themselves in me. But here I sit with people who believe in class warfare and the group.

The talk turns to current events. Ronald Reagan has just become the US president.

Larry Safarik says, "We need radical change. More than ever Communism remains the best hope of the human race."

I'm stunned. I say, "What about Isaac Babel and Mandelstam? What about the Gulag?"

"Bo-ring."

I've hurt my foot, slammed it hard against the side of a cage of mail. I go up to the sixth floor to see the nurse. In her little examining room, she tells me to sit and take off my shoe and sock. I do so. She sits in front of me and lifts up my foot and holds it in her hands. Then she looks at me.

"Your foot is filthy."

"What?"

"It's filthy. The back of your heel is crusted with dirt. When was the last time you washed it?'

I look at her. "Not long ago."

"You didn't do a very good job."

"I tried," I say, but I think: No, I didn't.

I feel ashamed. I've become a postie. I have the dirty heels of a PO4.

I'm talking to Sharon and enjoying it. Her feelings flush to the surface as easily as a seven-year-old's, and it doesn't surprise me that she's so close to the gay men in the plant.

"How was your trip?" I ask.

She's just come back from a long trip with Roland to his home town, a small place in Manitoba close to an Indian Reserve. Roland's oldest sister—he's the youngest of five kids, estranged from them all, facts that remind me of my own experience—his oldest sister has died of a heart attack. Roland begged Sharon to go with him to the funeral.

Sharon says: "It was sad. Roland tried to tell his mom he's gay. She acted as if she didn't hear him. He was his usual self though. The only picture he took was of two horses fucking."

I laugh. "He's your friend."

"Oh, I love him. He's the person in the world I feel most at ease with. I don't know if I'm a fag hag. I don't think so. Maybe."

She sorts. After a while she says: "But he's so selfish. If we're drinking and a man walks by, his eyes instantly turn to him and if he gets a signal then he's off. He'll just leave me there.

"And he's a tramp," she adds. "He'll fuck anyone. He goes out on the trails, he goes down to Boystown, he'll dress like he's a kid in tight jeans and short-sleeved plaid shirts and white socks and runners, but he's thirty-four. He'll let anyone pick him up."

A few weeks later—it's 1984, and Roland has HIV—I see him in the Castle, near the back, standing by the jukebox. He looks shrunken. Seeing him like that I know he's reached the stage where all that matters is finding his way to a bed. I know, too, that that stage, in which his life is focused solely on the present, is what he's after.

It's the Christmas rush. The fourth floor is filled with rows of cardboard cases. In front of each case stands a bewildered casual, blinking in the chaos. Agnes, the oldest of the part-timers, a monster of a woman who stands less than five feet tall and who has a mustache and fanatic eyes, is screeching at one of them: "YOU STOLE MY STOOL! YOU STOLE MY STOOL! I'LL KILL YOU! I'LL BREAK YOUR LEG!"

The man—the boy actually—lightly puts his hand on her arm. "Hey lady—"

Agnes pretends to fall. On her hands and knees, she starts to scream. The scream—a piercing sound, with bludgeoning undertones—brings the plant to a halt.

The boy bends down.

She sinks her strong yellow teeth right through his pants.

"You fucking bitch!"

"HE'S KILLING ME! HE'S KILLING ME!"

She bites him again.

We're working on the culling belt. Five or six people stand in line facing a moving belt that carries what's known as raw mail. Each of us picks out the bundled letters, parcels, keys, magazines, special deliveries and garbage, so that nothing drops off at the end of the belt except letters. Like most of the jobs in the post office, the work is automatic. To pass the time we talk.

Tonight the subjects are TV programs and childhood. In each case we use the same approach

We start with TV. We first remember the names of characters, the names of the shows, the years they appeared, the specific quality of their humour; we remember Jack Benny crossing his arms and looking at someone, how the Beverly Hillbillies talked, how Ed Sullivan would introduce those clowns and families of trapeze artists. Then Eleanor Rowe (a big fat prissy woman who thinks we should call the male supervisors "Sir" and who therefore often sorts alone) starts telling us how she first saw a TV in

New Westminster when she came to the coast as a twelve-year-old, and how "they couldn't tear me away from Jack and Rochester"; this leads to another story, more elaborate and prefaced by the words, "That reminds me!" in which Jules Marchand tells us how he used to be fascinated by Bluto's wirebrush beard and how he searched with his mom for cans of spinach like the ones Popeye ate but could never find them; then Ruth tells a story, then Jules again, until finally the buzzer sounds and we all look at each other, astonished at how the time has flown.

I listen to them talk. The happiness I feel, at first a tickle of joy, grows enormous. It fills me completely. I remember that when I entered the post office, I was alone in the world and had no place that in any real sense I could call home. And I think: that must explain it.

I've gone with Milena to her place on Rose Street. Sometime during the night a cold front blows in. When we wake the first time the sky is so blue it looks purple. But by the time we finally step outside at around three-thirty in the afternoon it's clouded over. Milena dances in front of me, smiling; her Slavic cheeks are tinted pink from the cold. "Isn't this great?" she says. "It's gonna snow!" We decide to walk to work. Both of us are starting early.

By the time we reach Main Street my fingers are freezing. It doesn't matter: I don't want to let go of Milena's mittened hand. Because of my happiness, everything I see has a glamour around it. We seem to have entered an earlier era where we might hear horses clopping behind us. Men work in the winter twilight as far up the street as we can see. They lift crates of chickens, huge barrels of olive oil. Faded Chinese farmers shuffle by dragging sacks of rice.

We turn down Pender. The crowd pushes against us. In the growing dark snub-nosed men hawk vegetables in wooden bins slippery with spoilage. They shout at the shoppers and lift bloody fish that gleam in the hot bars of light coming from the stores. Cronelike women who are permanently bent over at the waist turn their heads sideways to see the greens. They sniff at yellowish sheets of dried fish while the vendors shout.

It starts to snow, a few flakes at first, then more heavily. Milena laughs as we walk through the crowds, pointing out old ladies spitting at the side of the sidewalk, beggars sitting beside caps, people selling things on green outdoor mats and plastic garbage bags. In the red snow falling in the neon, we watch a man with no nose sell fish and another man with rotting teeth call out prices.

We walk hand in hand up Pender Street then turn up toward the plant.

But as we approach Dunsmuir she lets go of my hand. Her hair is wet and her eyes are bright.

"We can't go into the plant together," she says.

"Why not?"

"Because. I don't want to. Okay? That should be good enough."

She goes up the escalator ahead of me. I follow a minute later. On the fourth floor I punch in and walk to my case. The plant has become the world; everything in it has significance, everything yields a marvellous pain.

One night I push through the heavy Homer Street doors along with Will the bagboy. He walks toward the escalator whispering to the small cat he carries inside his coat. Will is in his thirties, a tall, passive, timid man with black sideburns framing a small white face. Because of those sideburns, and because of the work apron he wears that hangs down to his heavy shoes, he looks like a Victorian copyist.

Just before we reach the escalator, the little cat sticks its head out of Will's pocket. I lean over and stroke its nose. Will looks at me. He seems to be studying me. Then he looks at his cat and murmurs, "Now, kitty. You know better."

I say goodbye to him at the entrance to the loading docks, then go up two more escalators to the fourth floor. Ascending, I think about how childishness and premature old age mingle in Will.

That night, around two a.m., I go down into the basement. In the far corner, in a silence broken only by the buzz of the fluorescents, I see Will sleeping in the fetal position on top of a three-foot-high pile of canvas bags. His cat is curled up behind his knee. And at the sight of this sleeping couple I feel such an encompassing awareness of how little life offers some people that I won't know anything like it again until nearly fifteen years later, when one rainy January night, walking down Seymour to catch the bus home, I pass by a doorway lit by the same sodium glare as the plant's basement. There an old alcoholic with an exploded nose and wet eyes sits sprawled on the sidewalk, his pants down revealing his splotched buttocks and poor naked genitals.

I'm an adult then; and as adults do, I keep walking. But now, studying Will, I'm young. And as I push my binny through the plant afterward, seeing people sitting on their stools with their heads slumped, or throwing parcels in curious slow motion, or just standing in front of a cage, bewildered, as if a thought has occurred to them, their tiredness so affects me that for a moment the plant feels like a church, its metal cages sanctified, the overhead fluorescents votive lights.

III

In August of my third year in the plant I came home from work one morning and opened my apartment door to the sound of the phone ringing. It was my sister Marie-Claire. I hadn't heard from her for awhile, and though it was strange to hear the phone so early in the morning, I was glad she'd called. I told her so. But she resisted this, sounding tired; then she began crying, hiccuping with tears.

"Marie-Claire, what happened?"

She groaned and said something indistinct. Then she told me that my brother Mike had killed himself.

The next morning I flew to the Seattle-Tacoma airport. There I met my dad who had flown in from Memphis. We rented a car and drove to Philo Oregon, which was where Mike had died four days earlier.

It was hot that day. The sky was a perfect blue, without a cloud in it; and when we parked in the driveway of the house and opened the doors of the air-conditioned car, the cooking afternoon heat enveloped us.

We unlocked the door of the small house and went inside.

Stifling heat, smelly air: the air conditioner was turned off.

In the small living room, lying on the back of a chair, I saw Mike's brown cordurey jean jacket. I noticed he had wrapped a piece of tin foil around the TV antenna.

On the kitchen counter, cans of food. Eight-track tapes.

We went into the bathroom. Mike had died there. He had

first sliced his wrists with a kitchen knife; then when that hadn't worked, he had sliced his throat and walked to the bathroom and stepped into the bathtub. Bood stains were everywhere. They lay on the floor and they covered the tub like large rust marks or rust-coloured ceramic paint that had dried and cracked.

Around six we drove to the police station. The officer in charge, a red-faced man with an enormous belly that pushed against his shirt so that it was as free of wrinkles as the skin of a balloon, looked at us with sad eyes. "You don't want to see him," he said. Then we went to a motel on the outskirts of Philo, just off the freeway. After eating and watching TV, we got into our separate beds, completely worn out.

That night I fell asleep at once; then I awoke. Lying in bed staring up at the strange ceiling with my arms crossed on my chest, I listened to my dad's breathing. The air-conditioned motel room was very dark. But through a crack in the heavy curtains I could see the light that came from the illuminated swimming pool in the courtyard outside.

I looked at my watch on the bedroom table. Just after eleven p.m. I thought of Sharon and Roland. If I'd been in the post office, I would have been sitting on my stool surrounded by people I knew, sorting letters.

I couldn't sleep. As quietly as I could, I dressed in the dark in my shirt and pants. I got the key from the dresser counter and went out the door in my bare feet and then outside to the pool.

After the cold motel room, the night air felt balmy. It was never like that in Vancouver. Your room might be warm at night, even hot from the day's sun, but outside at night it was always cool. I remembered that from when I had first returned to the city.

I sat in one of the webbed chairs by the pool and stared at the water. It was lit up from beneath by lights. An older woman was swimming back and forth at the deep end.

She saw me and waved and got out of the pool and walked over to the chair that held her towel and cigarettes and lighter. Her feet left dark prints on the cement. She pulled her chair over to mine and sat down, drying off her face.

"My excuse is my dog's shitting and vomiting," she said. "What's yours?"

She was about fifty, with a beleaguered face and underslept eyes. I immediately felt relaxed with her.

"Oh, I couldn't sleep," I said.

She tapped out a cigarette. I noticed she was smoking Kools. I remembered that menthol taste. She fired up up her lighter and the flame shot two inches into the air and lit up her face.

"You're not from around here," she said. "Where you from?"

"I'm from Canada. From Vancouver, British Columbia."

"Igloos."

"Yeah." I smiled.

She smiled back. "I been to Vancouver. I remember that Sylvia Hotel with all the ivy. That's a very cute place. So what brings you here? I'm here because I'm on the run. My husband beat me up just one too many times and that was it. He was dragging me by the hair across the floor and I thought to myself, Okay, that's enough. That was when I got this black eye. Anyway I emptied out our account and I took off with Pete."

"Is Pete your son?"

"My dog. He's my dog. I don't have a son. He's the one that's sick."

"What's wrong with him?"

"He's got no appetite control." She inhaled deeply and let smoke trickle out her nostrils. "I bought this garlic sausage from this place just outside of here. Up near Bremerton? A deli. Anyway, it's homemade sausage. It's very tasty. I bought ten dollars worth. Okay. The guy said it would keep. Well it didn't need to keep because Pete ate it all up and now it's coming out of both ends. He's sick as a dog. So why are you here?"

"My brother died."

She held the cigarette out, an oddly delicate gesture. "Oh no. I'm sorry for you! Was he much older than you?"

"No. He was younger."

"Oh jesus." She shook her head. "How'd it happen? You want a smoke?"

"Sure. Thanks. I haven't had a Kool for years.... I used to live in the States."

"Where'd you live." She leaned forward and fired up the lighter.

"In Houston Texas."

"What a shit hole. I been there. There is not a worse city in America. Except Indianapolis."

"I've never been there."

"Oh, it's a shit hole too, take it from me."

I laughed. "Okay, I will."

"What happened to your brother?"

"He killed himself. He cut his throat."

"Oh god. That's awful." She looked at me. Then she got up and put her damp arm around me and held it there for a minute. Then she sat back down. "Why? Why'd he do that?"

"Oh, there's a lot of reasons. We moved a lot. And my brother....He wasn't strong. And he did acid back when people were doing that and I think that triggered something in him. It was in Texas. Anyway, he wasn't the same after that."

"What d'you mean?"

"It's hard to say." I looked at the pool and leaned forward; then with a feeling of relief I started talking to her and it was as if a poison inside me was being drained away. "I remember talking to him one day when I went down to visit. I said, 'So how are you feeling?' He said, 'I don't know.' I said, 'What d'you mean, you

189

don't know? How do you feel?' 'I don't feel anything,' he said. 'I feel empty inside. There's nothing in me.' That scared me. My mom took him to a psychiatrist not long after that and the guy said he might have developed schizophrenic tendencies. Well, we didn't know what that meant."

She nodded and smoked. We looked at the pool.

"What happened then?" she said.

"I'm not sure. I had moved out by then. But they were moving around—not that we were poor or anything. Just the opposite really. My dad was doing good. He's a corporate guy. But, you know, with corporations you move."

She nodded.

"And the point about that is that those corporate enclaves—well, nobody knows their neighbours. Because they've all just moved in too. Or they're moving out. And the way those places are set up is there's no local stores, there's nothing like that. Anyway, Mike didn't have his driver's license, so he couldn't get out."

"Sure."

"Anyway, when he was twenty-five, they got him a job. It was here in Philo. He had his license then so they bought him a car. And they rented him a house. And my dad helped him get a job. And then they moved again. And then Mike."

I fell silent.

Softly, she said, "What."

"I don't know. For a while it seemed all right. But then last year Mike lost his job. And then, I think, he started staying in. He didn't go out. He didn't have any friends. He didn't have anywhere to go."

"No," she said. "I guess he wouldn't."

We looked out at the pool.

After a minute she said, "Your poor parents."

"Yeah. I'm here with my dad actually."

"How's he doing? Is he holding up?"

"It seems like he is. So far. He's sleeping right now."

"Good. You need to sleep. I should know."

I smiled. "Yeah."

She lit me a second cigarette, the flame lighting up her face, and we both smoked, looking out at the pool.

The second day my dad and I went to the post office. The clerk handed us a pile of my brother's mail. We took it from him and closed off Mike's address. Then we went outside and my dad went through it.

It was all bills—one VISA bill after another. Finally my dad started to cry.

I stared at him. The sight of his face swept through me like the sight of a car accident. We stood there in the hot sun, in the clean quiet suburb just off the freeway, and I felt the horror in the air.

But the moment passed; and that afternoon my dad and I drove to the beach.

On our way we went through a suburb where all the houses were new. No sidewalks. Nobody on the street.

Looking out the window, my dad said, "I always liked to move. For me, it's always been like starting a new life, going to a new place." His voice was soft, reflective.

I didn't want to fight. "Maybe so."

"Maybe so?"

"Yeah, maybe."

He stared at me. "You know, I wanted us to move for a better life, for a better place."

I whispered, "Let's just drop it, okay?"

We stopped at a McDonald's by the freeway and got some cheese burgers and Cokes. Around one in the afternoon we arrived at the beach. Heat and blue sky. We sat on the beach in the heat, there on the Oregon coast, and as we ate our food we looked at the ocean through the heat mist. It was open ocean. No islands lay out there—there was no sense of being sheltered by islands and bays. The ocean stretched out endlessly in the shimmering heat.

It had been years since I had sat this close to my dad. After a while he said: "What are you thinking?"

"Oh—just remembering."

"Remembering...."

"Yeah....Just this thing a while ago. I had lunch with mom."

"What was it?"

"Well, I'd sent her these books by Michel Tremblay. You remember that? It was when you were living in Atlanta. I sent her these books and she came up to Vancouver. I can't remember why. But anyway, she called me up and we decided to have lunch together. And I thought: Well, I'll bring her some more Tremblay books. I was quite excited then about those books.

"Anyway. We had lunch. I mentioned the Tremblay books I'd sent her. She hadn't liked him. So here I am with these new Tremblay books sitting on the table between us.

"She says: 'Why can't he write in *good* French?' We're in this nice restaurant and she looks around, I remember, at these fish swimming in a tank. She touches my hand and says: 'You wouldn't find people talking French like that in here.'"

My dad smiled a little and nodded.

"I say: 'But they're funny too, those plays. At least parts of them are. You can see that.'

"And she says: 'Well, if you can call that funny.' You know the way she talks, that brisk way, like she's brushing something off. She says: 'Me, I don't find all those unhappy people especially funny. And the dirt. My word, what a mouth that man must have!'

"I say: 'But that's how you talked. Isn't that true?'

"And then she clucks her tongue. You know that?"

My dad nodded.

"You know that sound? 'Oh—' she says, and she makes that clucking sound. 'Maybe—at times,' she says. 'But it's an *ugly* way to talk, all that *calice, ciboire*, my God! It's how poor people talk, people with no education. It's vulgar! When I was teaching you children French—or trying to,' she says— 'I never taught *you* to talk like that.'"

My dad was smiling. He put his arm around me.

"I say: 'But it's how I remember you talking.'"

"She says: 'I was never that bad! Never. I always wanted to speak good French. Bruce, why do you *exaggerate* like this?'"

My dad laughed.

"So I say: 'Then why do I always think of you when I read the plays?'"

We looked out at the ocean. The heat mist had thickened. After a while my dad said: "You often think about the old days?"

"I remember things. I remember mom told me once how when she was just little in Manitoba she'd lie in bed with her sisters and they'd all go through the Eaton's catalogue together."

"That's right. She told me that."

"Yeah. I remember she said they'd tell each other in French which outfits to wear and the adventures that would come with the new clothes—each of them dressing the other. She said they'd sit around a kitchen table that was as big as a battleship and hear stories from Uncle Paul about haunted ships and werewolves. And she said they'd read French books too, but she liked the English books most."

"That's right." My dad looked out at the ocean. After a minute he said, "She's come a long way from that old life."

"You have too."

The sun had travelled across the sky. We were in shadow now, a little cooler. My dad said: "What else do you remember?"

"Things. It's odd. I remember you had a cigarette-making machine. Remember that?"

"I do, yes."

"I remember it was about the length of a crib board. And you laid out the tobacco in the rubber part, and then you laid out the paper. I think it was about a foot long. Vogue paper, wasn't that right?"

"That's right. Good memory."

"Then you'd work the machine—" I made a gesture with my two hands. "And you'd end up with a long cigarette that you cut up. You taught me how to do it."

"Did I?"

"Uh huh, you did."

"Huh."

I used to make the cigarettes, remember? When I was small. Then I'd put them in a copper goblet that it was my job to polish."

"Oh yeah?"

"Yeah. I remember how it smelled. The copper smell and the smell of the tobacco."

My dad laughed. "There's a few things there you remember."

"I remember more than that….Then we moved."

"Yes. Yes we did. To North Vancouver."

"Yeah."

"What d'you remember about that?" my dad said.

"I remember you couldn't go into the bush. There were only miles of sidewalks."

"You didn't like the moving."

"No….I didn't mind it when we did it. Later I minded it."

My dad didn't say anything. After a minute he stood up and looked at me. "I think we should go now," he said.

For a few days back at work the fluorescent lights overhead gave me a headache. I read books, trying to understand what had happened to Mike. And one day I found this sentence in a book by Czeslaw Milosz: "The liberation of man from subjection to the market is nothing but his liberation from the power of nature, because the market is an extension of the struggle for existence and nature's cruelty, in human society."

One night in November, coming home from work, I looked in the window of People's Co-op Bookstore down at Richards and Pender. Pictures of Lenin, Stalin and Trotsky stood in the window. Propped-up books advocated communism and revolution. They were in black and red; their titles were angry, uncompromising.

I stared at them. And for the first and last time in my life I gave their dogmatism my assent. The sense of horror I felt then, as if some gross imperfection lay at the heart of things, was so strong it could only be assuaged by an idea at whose centre hatred boiled. I looked at the books and nodded.

Not long afterward I decided to become a shop steward.

7. Colin's Big Thing

I

My eighth year in the Post Office it rained heavily all through March and April. Streets flooded. The mountains disappeared, and the city seemed entombed.

One night at a union dance, standing just inside the door with my shoes, jeans and coat wet, I saw Milena looking at me. I hadn't talked to her for over a year.

She walked over.

"You're soaked."

"I'm all right."

"You wanna dance?"

"I don't dance."

She smiled. "Well then I'll find somebody else."

A few nights later, I was waiting in line at work to punch out. I heard a whisper in my ear: "You wanna get laid?"

We went to her place. After we got in the door she took off her coat; then she sat in the big armchair, her legs spread apart, staring at me. I sat in the smaller chair. I lit a cigarette. My mouth was dry, my heart pounding.

"Light me one."

"Okay."

I lit a second cigarette. I handed it to her. She took it, puffed on it a couple of times; then she stubbed it out in the glass ashtray on the floor. Then she went into the bathroom. When she came out she was wearing only a tight yellow tank top. It had crept up above her belly button. I could see her naked stomach, the dark triangle of hair, her naked hips and legs, solid and muscular.

She took off her tanktop and lay on her stomach on the bed. Her head was turned sideways, her mouth pressed into the mattress.

"I've been a bad girl."

"Yes, you have."

"I need to be spanked."

I hit her buttocks hard with the palm of my hand. Her back flushed.

Around this time—the last time, though I didn't know it, that I'd visit Milena—I started to have a recurring dream. I dreamt I was in a place that was like the Post Office but more complicated, with many rooms in it, and dark chutes up which I had to inch, and huge windows furred with dirt. Men and women drifted in these shadowy rooms and inched up the chutes; and I tried to talk to them. But they turned away. By the order book—which in my dream was huge, a wooden construction that towered above people's heads—small groups of postal workers stared at me then turned away and spoke to each other. Standing among them, the woman I loved smiled a smile like that of a Medusa.

In June of that year, Sharon and Roland's friend Andy started missing work. He would show up for a day or two; then he wouldn't be there. One night, sorting with me, he said: "Have you ever known love?"

"Yes, I have."

"I haven't. It's all I want. To love and be loved."

I said, "You mean you haven't found someone to love you, or do you mean you haven't loved anyone?"

"Oh, I've loved people. But no one's loved me back. It hurts to be lonely," he added.

Each time he showed up at work he seemed thinner. His cheeks collapsed; the cartilage in his nose became visible. In September he transferred to Victoria. Two months later Sharon heard the news: anaesthetized by gin and barbituates so that his eyes had lost the ability to see, Andy had jumped from the balcony of a friend's twelfth-storey apartment.

When I heard of his death I remembered the night we had talked. He'd been wearing his red shorts. As we talked he'd put a foot up onto his ledge of his case. All at once I could see his genitals. Such a disparity between Andy's words and deeds. Yet because he had so openly expressed his need for love, that glimpse of his testicles had seemed poignant, in the way of all awkward or inadvertant emotion.

On December thirty-first that year Sharon and Roland and I went to the bar of the Dufferin to drink in the New Year. We sat with drag queens, talking and laughing. Watching Sharon walk toward us in a tight dress that I found pleasing, Roland, his eyes sunken in his now-gaunt face, said: "She wants you to take her home."

"You think so?"

"I know so. And you should."

"Roland, it's complicated."

He smiled. "It's not that complicated."

That night I walked home with Sharon over the Granville Bridge. When we got to her place, she looked at me, her eyes bright. She took a deep breath. "You want to stay over?"

"I'd like to."

We went upstairs and crept into bed. Her two boys were

sleeping in their rooms.

In the morning the boys came into the bedroom, still in their pyjamas. Their faces were soft with sleep. They sat on the bed. The youngest boy had brought in his pet rat. He held it out to me. "You wanna pet Sniffy?" he whispered.

Sharon had come to the union meeting with her youngest son. She had agreed to drive me home. Now the meeting was over. But Sharon was laughing, talking with the other stewards as Milena would have done; and I felt the old sense of abandonment.

I slipped out and walked down Homer to the bus stop on Hastings.

Ten minutes later Sharon drove by with her son in the back seat. She waved and pulled the car over to the curb. I walked over. She opened the door. Her face was flushed.

"Oh, I'm so glad I found you! We've been looking all over for you!"

"Yeah, we have!" her son said.

In May, with the leaves on the trees at their fullest and greenest, Roland died.

I read Michel Tremblay's *Therese and Pierrette and the Little Hanging Angel*. And the book so went to my heart with its evocation of a Catholic childhood that I sent it to my mom. I hoped that this time she would see what I saw, remember what I remembered.

I wanted to please her. Her letters had become worried. My dad was sick. And his letters had also changed in tone. And then it became clear I had to visit: he had cancer.

On my third night in Redville Kentucky (where my mom and dad and my youngest sister Louise now lived) my mom and I got into an argument.

"You know Bruce," she said, "I was really quite upset when I read that part in *Therese and Pierrette*—"

"The Tremblay book."

"Yes. The one you sent. I was very upset by how he refers to the nuns. Very upset. Why did you send me that book?" She was looking away from me, her tight mouth trembling with unhappiness.

"Well—tell me," I said. "What part do you mean?"

"You know what part I mean. The part where he just goes on and on, and it's so unfair. I don't know why he would write like that. He really must hate the nuns because *nobody* would talk to a Mother Superior like that. It was all so *twisted* and *ugly*."

"Well, he was trying to make a point—"

"What point? Tell me what point!" She started to cry. "Oh, I get so tired of this. And tired of you. You don't write, you don't write, and then you send me a book that just makes me think of your Auntie Annette. And it's so unfair. You never met a gentler, kinder person than Annette. She's a wonderful nun."

"But mom," Louise said, "that's not the point. We all *know* Annette is a good nun. You're taking the book personally. And you're really being unfair to Bruce."

Later, after my mom had gone upstairs to tend to my dad, Louise and I went for a walk, down the winding street that led from the expensive suburbs on the Redville hills. In town the houses looked older. They were much smaller; and though we walked on sidewalks now (there were no sidewalks up in the hills, among the expensive houses), we walked alone. After a while we passed a fat man in jeans who sat on the porch of a two-room house watching a small child in diapers. We passed mobile homes. The driveways of the small houses were narrow as cart tracks; their pavement was cracked. A poor town, then, though the hills above were rich.

Walking back up the winding street in the gathering dark, we saw a person coming toward us.

Louise said, "That looks like mom….Yeah, it's her. Now I wonder what…."

We walked toward her. My mom was walking stiffly, her face rigid. As she came toward us she looked at us with pleading, hesitant eyes.

"Mom, are you okay?" Louise said.

My mom again started to cry. "I thought you'd left….I thought you were angry at me and had gone away….I felt so alone…."

Louise went up to her and hugged her. "Mom, we're not angry at you. That's wrong to think that….We love you…." She was stroking her, softly moving her arm up and down my mom's back, while the older woman, nearly a foot shorter than Louise, held her and wet her shoulder with her tears.

After a bit, my mom sighed and wiped her eyes and smiled at us. "Ah God I'm so ashamed….I'm sorry….I feel better now."

She took my arm and looked at me with tearful eyes. "Can you forgive me?"

I hugged her. "Mom, you're not at fault. If anybody's at fault I am."

"Ah well, let's not talk about fault," she said. "Come on. It's creepy out here on the street with no one out." She laughed. "And somebody might see me crying in front of my son who never comes home and put two and two together! Come on, let's go home."

We walked back up the street in the dark, past the huge houses with their flags flying in front of them.

Eight months later my dad lay dying in a hospital in Columbus Ohio.

One night walking down the hall of the hospital I saw

Luanne, his nurse.

"How's my dad?"

"Not so good, I'm sorry. He's hallucinating right now."

I went into his room. The black man who had the bed next to him had his back to my dad, turned away, trying to watch TV. My dad was shouting and muttering, strange phrases, names of his sisters and parents and places I hardly knew, sections of Winnipeg that went back sixty years. The pleading and imprecations poured out of him. In their intimacy and nakedness, in the way they laid my dad bare, they frightened me.

The man on the other bed said, "Man, he's havin a hard time. Can't watch TV with all that."

"I'm sorry."

"That's okay."

They were still feeding my dad. It was a brown liquid that went into his veins through a plastic tube. But he couldn't digest it, couldn't take it in. The stuff came back up the tube red with blood.

That night after falling asleep for a while, my dad came to consciousness and sanity. He tried to pull out the tube that was feeding him nutrients he couldn't absorb. He couldn't manage it. Then he started to weep. "I know what's going on," he said. "*I know.*"

He lay back, his eyes in his skeletal face blurred with tears. His hair was damp with sweat. To soothe him I leaned over his high bed and hugged and kissed him. I felt his bristle; how many years it had been since I had felt my dad's bristle on my face! Not since early childhood. We had never hugged or kissed. Later I realized that my memories of him as a physical being were all from when I was a small boy in Hinton. We had bathed together; I remembered his laughter, his cigarette breath, his big soft warm hands, his cock and balls, so big compared to my hairless child's penis, and the same shock of his bristle on my face when he had picked me up and kissed me and I had screamed with delight at being lifted up in the air from my bath.

That night in the hospital I leaned forward and put my arms around him and kissed him. "That's okay, dad," I said. "That's okay." I held him and rocked him and kissed him again.

Two days later he died. A week later, at the Redville Catholic Church, I and my youngest brother Paul and two men from the church carried the coffin up to the altar. I felt (in that strange town, in that country not my own) that I was playing a role. I felt I wasn't myself, as I would have been back in Vancouver. Instead I was an actor taking on the role of a man responsible and burdened; and I tried to do my best. I suppose Paul felt and did the same.

The priest spoke. I should have said something. But I was too alienated. I sat in the front pew with my mom and my sisters and brother listening to the banal words of this man who had never spoken to my dad except at Sunday mass. I looked around. Apart from us and the pallbearers, only two neighbours and a couple of men from dad's company were there.

My mom moved to Denise Creek, near Parksville, on Vancouver Island. In Christmas of 1990 Sharon and I came to visit.

On Christmas Day we sat at the kitchen counter, drinking coffee and talking. Marie-Claire sat at the counter next to Sharon and my mom and me; across from us sat Louise and Annette and Paul.

"My parents used to come to Denise Creek," Sharon said. "They'd drive over, then have a nap in the car. It was an old Nash Rambler. They loved to fish, my mom especially."

"Oh, I loved to fish too," my mom said. "And Mike. But your dad was too impatient." She touched Paul's arm. "Like you, dear."

She smiled; as usual, her eyes had filled with tears, mentioning Mike. But they weren't tears of grief. Time had altered that.

"Oh, Bruce," she said, looking at me. "I have a book of photos I want you to see."

She groaned as she got up from the counter—"Oh god, my back"—and then returned with a large book whose title was *Et la riviere coule toujours 1890-1990. And the River Flows Always.* She said: "I was—I told you about this, don't you remember? Sharon, isn't he awful the way he doesn't listen—anyway, I was at the big reunion in Pine Falls with all your relatives. There were hundreds of us there. And they did this book."

She placed it out in the middle of the counter so we could all see and started turning the pages.

"You see how the people go back eh?" She pointed to a picture of people in front of a sod hut. 'When I was a little girl people lived in places like that. They taped sheets to the roof to keep the bugs from falling. Isn't that awful? But you know, it wasn't as bad as it sounds. When your dad and I got married we lived in a cabin like that on our honeymoon and we had a wonderful time."

I said, "I've got a picture of you in my wallet from then."

"Can I see it?"

"Sure."

I took it out and put it on the kitchen counter beside the open book. My sisters and brother looked at it.

"God, mom, you were beautiful!"

"You were!"

"Look at that coat."

My mom, smiling a little, looked at herself appraisingly. "Not too bad. You should have seen your dad then. So handsome….He was always sure of himself," she added. "I had lots of boyfriends I can tell you, but John was different. He said to me, 'In the Navy I learned what I wanted to do.'"

Paul said, "He joined the Navy young."

"He joined in 1941. He was sixteen. Tall for his age. He was in the North Atlantic convoy. A friend of his was killed, washed overboard in a storm. He worked as a stoker."

"During the war was when he learned to hate the British," Paul said.

"Well…that's a little strong," my mom said. "He hated their condescension to Canadians. The way they wouldn't let enlisted men into certain places, only officers. Your dad detested the class system in England, and he detested it here."

Louise said, "Is that why we moved to the States?"

"In part, yes," my mom said. "Your dad always liked Americans for their openness. It was as far back as the war that he started to like them. Your dad had a big chip on his shoulder because he was Polish. And in those days with dumb Polack jokes it was serious. In Canada, if you were a Pole you were stupid. A hunkie. God, John hated that!"

"Dad never liked Polish jokes," Paul said.

"Your dad liked no ethnic humour…And of course he was so unhappy at home."

Marie-Claire said, "I remember when we went to visit his parents in Winnipeg. Jesus, that was just so awful."

"When was that?" I said.

"Don't you remember, dear?" my mom said. "It was when we were living in Allenby and we took our big trip to Pine Falls."

"I remember the trip," I said. "But I don't remember visiting dad's parents."

"Well, no, you wouldn't! That's because you stayed in Pine Falls with Aline and them! You remember?"

I nodded, though I didn't remember. "So the rest of the kids stayed with dad's parents."

Marie-Claire said, "That's right. And it was *awful.* When we walked up, dad's mom was washing the front steps. God. She hadn't seen dad for over twenty years. And she just looked up and said, 'Hello Johnny,' and she went back to washing the steps. *Jesus.*"

"It was terrible," Annette said. "Dad started crying. I'd never seen him cry before."

Paul said, "It was different with mom's side of the family. They were friendly. I especially remember that trip to Pine Falls."

"Oh yes, they were very friendly. When you were in Powerview—you remember, it was like a little suburb of Pine Falls—it was like it was our town. It was almost all Vincents. But people have left."

Now my mom moved the big book toward her. Slowly, taking her time, she started tracing out a great migration that had dispersed the people she had grown up with to the four corners of the continent.

"You see here, Roger Lemilen and his wife? Well, they lived in Powerview for almost thirty years. But then Roger got cancer, so they moved to Winnipeg and Roger died and Claire moved to Tucson....

"The Brochiers. Let's see. Claude Brochier. Oh, god, where did they....Oh I remember....They moved to Edmonton, that's right. She died there. I always wanted you to visit them. Bruce, do you remember your uncle Claude from Hinton? He wasn't really your uncle, but...."

"I do. I remember one day at a wedding in the hotel he fed me raisin tarts. I was sitting under the table."

Paul said, "Raisin tarts. Yum yum."

My mom stared at him. "Are you hungry? Eat. Eat. Eat. Oh, dear, that wasn't Claude! That was your uncle Denis! My brother! He was drunk that day. Oh god. He was a good man. He was so kind. I remember when your dad drove us back to Hinton in the new station wagon, Denis said he didn't know how anybody could drive such a big car."

"What about Uncle Michel?" Louise said.

"Oh, he was wild. People said he was part-Indian. I *hated* that. But it was what people said then. If you were French, the bigshots in town didn't give you the time of day. I hated that smalltown mentality. But that was the way it was. It was a preju- dice…." My mom looked at me. "Michel married Therese, you remember? She treated him bad. He adored her. She ran around but he kept taking her back. And then, I think he was hoping it would settle her down, they moved to…oh, Leduc, that's right, in Alberta. It didn't settle her down though."

My mom stared at the book, smiling, remembering. A small snort came from her, then the innocent tears. "I loved Michel. He was my youngest brother. I was heartbroken when he died."

Like a person playing solitaire, she slowly traced out one per- sonal history after another. Then she fell quiet. She sighed, and closed the book. She turned to us, her face composed. "Well, you see how it is."

II

In my sixteenth year of working for Canada Post I at last managed to transfer out of the plant to Postal Station K at Nanaimo and Hastings.

Part-time work now, starting at one in the afternoon; and on those long, sunny fall days, the station quiet, my few jobs finished by four-thirty, I feel I've come to a terminus in my life.

That spring Sharon and I start *The Vancouver Review*. Pushed by that, and thinking about my mom, the great dispersal of people which has shaped her life and my own, I start to make notes on yellow pads of paper about times gone by and the things that have happened to me.

One afternoon in December Murray Smith turns to me while I'm stacking householders by his case. He flips a finger up and down.

"You know Colin Upton?"

"Never heard of him."

"He draws comic books. You should read him. You'd like him. I've got a couple in my locker. I'll lend them to you."

That evening I go through the books—each called *Colin's Big Thing* and each a collection of stories with Upton himself as their main character. The comics grip me. As if I'm seeing them in a distorted or darkened mirror, the scenes Colin depicts, though they're not the same, remind me again and again of Alistair's. And by the time I'm finished I know I want to get something by Colin into the *VR*. And I want to meet him.

A few days later I head out. The Fraser Street bus is late. The digital clock at Cambie has told me it's eleven below zero and now small flakes of snow are twisting down. I can feel the bitter cold in my chest and on my face. I've brought a small pile of comics for Colin to look at, and though it's hard to concentrate in the extreme cold, I flip through one with a bare hand —issue #1 of *Teenage Mutant Ninja Turtles.*

A black teenager of about fifteen lounges up to the stop. He wears a red toque that makes his dark face vivid. He jumps onto the bench, his feet making skidmarks in the mangy nap of snow. He jumps down, turns sideways and kicks a leg out to just in front of the bus stop wall. He flings an arm out with the knuckles turned in. He whips around and, adding new skidmarks, again jumps onto the bus stop bench. Then he jumps down and says:

"Hey, mister, you really read comics?"

"Sure," I say.

"No way."

"Absolutely."

"No way. What do you like most."

I think a moment. "I guess I like Scrooge McDuck most. And some of the Marvel comics."

"No way." He spins around, kicks out to the side again. "*I* write a comic. I got my own superhero. I designed the costume when I was fourteen. Yeah, and I've written away to Marvel in New York. See what they gotta say."

"Oh, yeah?" I admire his brass. "That's interesting."

"No way." The boy leaps onto the bench. "You're kinda *old* to be reading comics aren't you?"

"Well, I don't know. Maybe."

"Yeah, well, maybe not, maybe not."

It's hard to concentrate—my whole body is shaking—but we talk about the Marvel artist Jack Kirby anyway. Then the bus rolls up. It skids into the curb, seeming larger than normal in the freezing air. "I gotta go," I say, walking with relief toward the half open door. "It's been nice talking to you. Good luck with New York."

"No way," the boy says. Then, aware that the phrase doesn't make sense just there, he grins at me. "Have a good day, mister!"

I'm early. When I get off at the Fraserview Cemetery I step into whirling snow. I can sense it underfoot. Thick flakes land on my cheeks. I feel that exhilaration that comes when you walk out into the carnival world of unusual weather. I've decided to visit Alistair's grave, something I haven't done in fifteen years.

With the snow on the ground, it takes me a while to find it. The gravestone is set in the grass, a black marble rectangle which, when I brush off the snow, I see is chipped, the inscribed letters filled with moss. Incised on each side of the letters, but blurred now almost to the point of invisibility, are two symmetrical drawings of a cherub or child holding a paint brush. The inscription reads:

Alistair Fraser
1951 - 1972
Forever in our Hearts

I walk through the cemetery then up Fraser. The dark turbans on the men and the coloured saris on the women—this is the Sikh part of town—stand out.

On Chester Street I go down some steps on the side of an old house—steps already covered with more than an inch of snow. And at the bottom of the steps I open the unlocked basement door.

Immediately I feel a powerful sense of familiarity. In the basement laundry is washing. *Slop, slop; slop, slop*—that old sound, there in the dimly lit room. A sense of imminence takes hold of me; and as I walk through the basement toward the open door that leads to Colin's living room, the smells of damp concrete and soap and steamy air which I haven't known for so long sharpen that sense of imminence until all at once I feel as I did all those years ago when I watched Cate, wearing only her slip, bent over a wringer-washer doing our clothes.

Colin himself I'm not prepared for. Half consciously I've been expecting Alistair, or someone like him. Instead I confront a giant dressed in shorts and a tee shirt who looms in his chair across from me like a ponderous boy. A nervous shyness constantly kindles in his eyes and dies down, kindles and dies down. After looking carefully through the books I've brought him, he says in a cockney accent put on to mask his anxiety: "You want to see *moy* comics?"

Looking through them, I'm especially struck by the drawings of Colin as a child. What grief they express. A bellowing mouth stretches open in a black bat wing of anger; a scrunched-up face turns ugly with pain. And the accompanying words, with their child's plainness, contribute to the drawings' eloquence:

> *Growing up I suffered from severe emotional problems: depression and tantrums.*
>
> *I thought I was bad. I fought hard to keep my emotions inside but they eventually exploded out anyway.*
>
> *I can vividly remember my mother yelling at me, "Do you want to be put in an insane asylum?! Because that's where you're going!!!"*
>
> *For years I expected to be locked up.*
>
> *When I saw derelicts downtown I thought booze made them crazy, crazy like me, and I feared I'd become one of them.*

The emotions that produced that sorrowing child seem to permeate Colin's room. In an odd way—in a way that startles me, so that my eyes prickle with tears—the room reminds me less of Alistair than of Ray and Jeannine. It's crammed with things; on the wall opposite me I notice a baroque mat of caps and hats and military jackets. Postcards and tacked-up pieces of paper cover every surface as if to provide a kind of necessary insulation. One of these pieces of paper catches my eye; it might have filled a zoomed-in panel in one of Alistair's Mrs. Nemo stories:

THINGS TO DO IN CASE OF ANXIETY
1. Drink herb tea.
2. Go for a walk.
3. Call a friend.
4. Masturbate.

Colin coughs nervously. I look up from his comics and smile to reassure him. "They're great."

"Well, I'm glad you think so." He speaks slowly, in the toneless voice of a deeply anxious man positioning himself far from his interlocutor.

We sit still for a moment. Then in the same toneless voice: "Would you like some cookies?"

"Sure."

Colin goes into the kitchen to get them. I wait for him in the darkening room watching the snow fall outside the window. Dander or some other allergen hangs in the air. My eyes fill. I blink the tears away. A small wood beetle of a kind I'm familiar with in my own apartment crawls up the wall near the couch. Colin's cat Walrus stares at it. His ears prick forward. I too become engrossed in watching the beetle; and somehow its small life seems to join with the life in the comic books on my lap that because of the growing dark are becoming hard to read.

A few weeks later Granville Street huddles under the shadowless light of Vancouver on a day when the rain is falling.

It's cold. Three teenage panhandlers lie together on a wet sleeping bag near the Capital 6 Theatre. A crazy man with eyes nearly shut from bruises and scabs on his face walks back and forth in a rage. This portion of Granville appears often in Colin's comics and now it looks as black and white as when he draws it.

"So," he says, leading me up to Golden Age Collectibles, "you want to go in and see the competition?"

"Okay."

I open the door—a man in my forties—and once again in Colin's presence I feel touched by a ghost. Who is it? I don't know. I think it's Alistair, though I'm not sure. But as Colin and I pass through the darkened doorway, something grabs me; and just for an instant the street jumps around and I have a vision of Vancouver as it was twenty years before, with its round-nosed buses and skies like smoke.

The vision preoccupies me to the point where I feel alarmed. And when Colin says, "What do you think?" I shake my head.

But I look around. And still caught up in my hallucination, the first thing I think is that the number and variety of comics has increased unbelievably since those long-ago days when Alistair and I used to talk about them on Adanac Street.

Row after row of comics line the long tables, thousands of them, separated by cheap cardboard dividers that have been written on with a felt pen, as if the business was growing so fast the owners couldn't keep up. The Klondike atmosphere that now permeates Granville has spilled out of the sex shops and video arcades further up the street and rolled through the door. Splatter movie posters hang in long racks, a seven-foot-tall image of Batman stares cross-eyed from the display window—and the concrete floor, the dim light, the sword and sorcery magazines full of naked women kneeling with their heads bowed before enormous men carrying battle axes—it all has that humid atmosphere that I associate with Willy's Dirty Books and the Midnight Star Video Arcade where men step into small black booths at the back and ejaculate onto the floor.

There are no girls; and the boys are mostly young men, whose relationship to the material in front of them has the same quiet-eyed obsessiveness that you see in someone looking for a certain kind of porno. Partly because of my mood, it unnerves me watching an anxious boy who looks about twelve and weighs maybe eighty pounds discuss *The Punisher* with a man in his twenties who wears insectlike sunglasses and a long black leather jacket down to his boots.

I lift my chin toward the two. Colin nods. "Fanboys. I can't stand them. I just *hate* that superhero crap."

To provoke him I pick up a copy of one of Todd Macfarlane's books. Macfarlane grew up in BC and he's had a huge success—his first *Spiderman* book was the best selling comic in history, selling millions of copies in just a few days.

I hold the book out. "What do you think?"

I expect dismissal. Instead, with the careful, remote honesty which is an aspect of his shyness Colin pins down what I also feel is weak in Macfarlane's work. "His comics are very stylish, but there's no story. And his art's not that great. He used to sit on his bed in Sapperton in New Westminster imitating Jack Kirby."

"Not a bad model."

"That's not the point. Macfarlane's part of the last two generations that's learned to draw from comics themselves—they lack the fundamentals that a broader art education might've given them. The work is a little unreal; but that's part of the stylishness."

I nod. It's poignant to hear Colin dismissing this comic book superstar. I flip through the book and show him an especially lurid spread. Tight closeups balloon into a dark cityscape. The colours are like candy. There are no words.

"This is at the heart of things now," I say.

He takes the open comic and looks at it. He shakes his head. I notice the hairs on his chin, his anxious eyes, and remember my friend Bob Shermanowski (who knows him slightly) telling me about all the years Colin lived alone with his mom. "Yeah, maybe," he says now. "But I can't stand this stuff. It's pure consumerism. And it's always the same. Story after story after story. It never changes."

"So how did you get started in comics?"

But he's caught, studying Macfarlane's art. Then he looks up at me nervously and gathers himself and begins talking. He speaks slowly. His voice is again nearly toneless, and suddenly I have a sense of myself as Rip van Winkle, as if I've been asleep for the past two decades and have now woken to a world in which people talk differently than they did before. Colin's toneless way of speaking didn't exist when Alistair and I used to discuss comics. And during all my time in the post office I never heard it. I feel the dust of years on my skin.

"A lot of what I began doing," Colin says, "had to do with the fact that I thought superhero comics were crap. I had a pretty elitist attitude about comics. The American stuff I thought was kid stuff. But the European stuff—" and now irony enters his voice, distancing him from his own enthusiasm— "it came out in hardback, it was graphic novels!"

He sighs. "The level of craft was just so much better. The whole European art style—the style in *Tin Tin*, say—was fascinating. It was so calm and detailed."

He carefully shuts the comic. In a distant, exhausted, almost effete voice, he says, "And I was interested in the historical references in the comics. American comics were just unending soap operas; I didn't have either the strength, the money, or the inclination to collect the whole series to find out what happened."

We walk around the store. I point to *The Dark Knight*

Returns. "I think Frank Miller is a great popular artist."

"He's a fascist," Colin says.

"What a moralist you are!"

"Moi?" He smiles.

We go deeper into the store, pulling comics out of the racks and flipping through them. To each comic we devote a phrase or a couple of sentences. And as we do this our relationship to each other changes. It's as if our touching and flipping through the books brings them to life and allows their slim-waisted heroes to step out of the pages. A feeling of being protected and at home comes over us.

Colin starts to relax. The background noise diminishes. Our conversation quickens. It becomes decisive, emphatic—quick, short bursts of communication. We've turned into fans.

"Harvey Pekar. He was the big influence."

"*American Splendor.*"

"A great comic."

"And *Raw* magazine."

"Edited by Art Speigelman. Who drew *Maus.*"

"That's an amazing book."

"Do you know Ben Katchor's stuff?"

"Julius Knipl. One of the *great* characters."

Warmed up now, Colin talks about punk rock and the fanzines associated with it and how they influenced him. "Their stuff made it seem like *you* could do stuff." He stares at a man in his mid-thirties buying what look like Battletech figures. "I used to collect those," he murmurs.

Then he goes back to his earlier point. "The material in mainstream American comics is so fatuous, so lacking in any real story, that you have to work hard to keep up interest. Most of the independents I know are into storytelling—they don't have the flashy effects. I think that this has a lot to do with the influence of punk rock in Vancouver. Its influence has been huge here. With alternative comics, like alternative music, you have to *say* something. This makes it more relevant to Generation X and younger people. There's a desire for less ambiguity—so many things in modern society disguise their real message. So younger people now, their idea is, 'If you want to say something, *tell me*, don't hide it in metaphors or incomprehensible imagery that I can't understand.' I don't think this means people are ignorant. It's just that their knowledge is not about Keats."

It's a lot for him, all these words. Colin becomes silent. We drift through the store, then back out onto the street.

Rain is pouring down. A friend of Colin's walks up to us under a black umbrella, a young Asian man with bad skin.

"Hey Colin. You going to the opening tonight?"

"I don't know. I moight."

The cockney has returned. Colin stares at his friend, his big coarse face registering worry, curiosity, shyness and a muffled aggression. He seems formidable, standing there on the sidewalk in the pouring rain.

III

Bob Shermanowski is sitting behind the counter of Caliban Books, looking something up on the computer. The beige plastic of the terminal is filthy. His eyes on the screen, Bob says, "What did you think of him?"

"Well, he's very gentle….And he's anxious."

"Like Neil." Neil is a poet who works in the store from six p.m. to midnight.

"A little, maybe. He's way more imposing, though. Actually he can make you uncomfortable."

"Because he's so big." Bob's eyes remain on the terminal.

"A little bit that, yeah. But it's also he's got so much anger in him. He's a moralist."

Bob looks up. "What do you mean?"

"Oh, just he hates what he calls 'flashy effects.' What did he say to me? 'So many things in society disguise their real message!'"

At once I feel ashamed. Because I respect this aspect of Colin—it's deeply felt. But it's also part of the heaviness, the provinciality that ties him down like a self-constrained Gulliver. At times Colin reminds me of the Odlum street poets, and even more of a couple of overweight shop stewards I knew in the post office. They too usually seemed shy. They'd walk around, these big men, with folded *Province* newspapers sticking up from the back pockets of their jeans, and they'd stare at the supervisors standing on the docks with a hatred so great I sometimes mistook it for sadness.

Colin's own anger flows from his relationship to Vancouver. One afternoon when we're walking down Robson I ask him about it. He tells me he loves the city.

I'm surprised. "So you don't think there's any problems with Vancouver?"

"Nope."

"Really?"

"I like it here." Colin moves his hand at the bumper-to-bumper traffic going past. "I like Vancouver's tolerance. I like the rain." Then, switching to his cockney accent: "I quoit like the punk rock bands."

I nod; I accept this. And when we sit down in the Robson Kitto and I look at the books he's brought, the fantasy he wants me to see jumps out from the very first page. I look with delight at a map he's drawn of the country he inhabits within Vancouver itself—a place with its own distinctive people, history, uniforms and flag. The enclosed, stamp-collector quality that marks so much of Colin's work makes this map irresistible—looking at it, I seem to look into the heart of his life.

But like his dismissal of Macfarlane, the map also expresses something poignant. Colin wants to present Vancouver as a fairy tale world—yet plainly the city has in many ways harmed him. Vancouver judges Colin and Colin accepts its judgement; and so the almost unconscious judgements he makes in return are marked by furious hurt instead of the malicious laughter that would give him a bigger readership.

Still, how much this damaged city mouse sees and feels! As I sit there in Kitto reading his books, characters float up from their pages and surround me: gargoyle-like derelicts, men who are weaklings and sexual cowards, desperate gays, women so stridently self-righteous that when they speak their faces twist with anger as if with a cramp. Conformity and inarticulate resentment float in the faces of the thirty-year-olds that Colin's alter ego hangs out with. Though few of them drink, when they ride the buses at night a river of alcohol flows through the aisles.

In some of Colin's stories, night and booze combine to produce a psychological landscape that wouldn't be out of place in Moscow. In this colonial city people sit speechless on the bus, immobile among the afterimages of American movies that in comparison make them seem barely alive, not speaking to the squealing girls from Hong Kong or the heroin addicts trying to sell them their coats. It's a frozen city, full of men and women unable to talk to each other, a town so killingly inward that anything emotionally showy gets met with rage.

This is the city I came back to in 1970. It astonishes me to see it. And the work reflects the man. Sitting across from me Colin eats quickly, almost desperately. He doesn't speak. I can see anxiety in his eyes.

What can I say to him? What topic can I bring up? The unease that marks those who have been mentally ill hangs around him like an atmospheric disturbance.

About a week later I call him up to ask about a review he's drawing for the magazine.

"How's it going, Colin?"

"Okay." His voice is a dull, toneless whisper.

"What's wrong?"

"Oh, nothing. I might lose my apartment, that's all." He can hardly speak.

"What happened?"

"A flood."

"That's terrible."

"I guess."

Listening to him is like listening to a child who knows intimately the pain that's to come. All his defenses have unravelled. And at that moment it becomes clear to me why Colin is so open to the atmosphere of Granville and Fraser Streets and why their grey skies and ugly, anxious faces have imprinted themselves so plainly on his books.

"What do you see in him?"

Bob Shermanowski and I are in Caliban Books, strolling the literature aisle.

"He's vulnerable. He reminds me of Vancouver."

"He reminds you of Vancouver." Bob shakes his head. "What does *that* mean?"

One evening walking off the sea bus on the Vancouver side, I see Colin moving ahead of me through the crowd. He's wearing combat boots, dark fatigues, a long black coat, a military hat and a black and white Yasser Arafat scarf wrapped around his neck. He moves like a big John Cleese, revealing with every step a held-in truculence. An air of imposing eccentricity radiates from him. As he walks with the others over the railway tracks, he looks out at the sodden clouds and the warehouses whose dirty windows faintly reflect a seaplane taking off. At that moment, under the walkway's garish light, with night coming on, I see in Colin a distillate of the fantastic city that I see in my dreams, a kind of compound of fog and rain and grey and darker grey clouds in which Alistair wanders the streets, a ragged nobleman who looks at me with pitying contempt, and Cate walks past me down a hallway that smells of the remote past while around us drift World War Two Canuck soldiers in scratchy uniforms.

Two weeks later, I'm sitting in Colin's room looking at a portrait he's recently drawn. Battling the self-erasure that leads him to present a "gentle" front to the world, Colin has sketched himself in red and acid green as a naked Satan, muscular, rigid with energy, his cock erect, his mouth a shock wave of aggression.

"This is terrific."

"You think so?"

"Yeah. It shows you as you are. You ought to do more things like this. Laugh at the world."

But how hard such laughter is for Colin. I realize this as I look at the two recent stories he wants me to see, "Nightmares" and "I'm Not Angry Anymore."

"Nightmares," which is painstakingly—even painfully—drawn with whiteout on black-inked panels, is probably the best thing I've seen by him. In the story it's 4 A.M. Colin lies on his bed, lacerated by self-loathing. His face is uglier and more adult than usual. The narrative lettered onto one of the blackened panels reads, "It's one of those nights when I feel the urge to call everyone I've ever met and apologize to them for having inflicted my odious presence on them." And in the large opening panel for "I'm Not Angry Anymore" Colin names in heavily inked letters all the things that torment him about himself: "FAT. TALENTLESS. UGLY. LOUD. SMELLY. USELESS. STUPID. LOSER. PERVERT. GREEDY. INCONSIDERATE."

The two stories are awkward. They seem graceless. But I'm shaken by them. Precise without being self-pitying, they so clearly express this big, strange man's sensitivity to his city's rigid social control that the exhausted sadness with which they end stays with me for days.

One afternoon that spring when we're walking down Chester toward 49th, I ask Colin: "Why do you draw comics?"

"I can't answer that question."

We turn onto 49th. I say, "Okay then, why do you draw 'true-life' comics?"

Colin thinks for a moment. "I want to produce a record of the Vancouver I know before it disappears forever."

And there it is. I feel immediate assent.

Colin adds, "That's why I take photographs. I go out and I

photograph things so I'll remember how they look."

A chill of excitement crawls up my back. "What kind of things?"

"Oh—lamp posts. People's jackets….Faces."

"That's interesting. A friend of mine used to do that. He used to draw comic books too."

"What's his name?"

"Alistair Fraser."

"Never heard of him."

"No, he's dead."

Slowly and carefully, Colin says, "I'm sorry to hear that."

A week later we're again sitting in his room.

"You want to see one of my early comics?"

"Okay."

Colin hands me a mini-comic, "Self-Portrait #1," done when he was in his early twenties. It's a self-published booklet that's roughly the size of the *Little Archie* books you can find in Chinese grocery stores.

Pointing to a panel in this little book, Colin says, "This is what I used to look like."

The panel shows him drawing a comic-book page, calm-eyed, softer-faced than I'm used to, wearing fingerless wool gloves, his hair in a little ponytail. The tiny block-lettered text that fills over half the panel reads like a confession:

My Bloody Comics

Ive been self-publishing mini-comics for about 4 years, producing over 60 comics plus work for other publications with critical praise from small press fanzines. I hope to break into "pro" comics soon. I believe strongly in comics as a legitimate means of personal expression unburdened by artistic pretensions, with untapped potential. I find it

*distressing when people dismiss comics as "kids stuff" I
hope to help change this perception. I know Im not very
good yet but Im determined to keep at it and expand my
readership. When I'm cartooning is one of the few times
when I dont feel awkward or stupid. If you want to know
more about me, read my damn comics!*

Early work. Yet already Colin's mixture of diffidence and
honesty comes through. Things haven't turned out as the young
artist had hoped, though, and almost ten years after this piece, sitting across from me in the room featured in so many of his
comics, Colin rocks back and forth in angry grief. "It seems hope-
less. People are enthusiastic about comics, but as far as getting
anywhere it's like being on hold. You get a feeling you're never
going to break out. Most of the older guys have had to give up
comics and get real jobs to support their families. And the
younger guys—well, they just can't get *anywhere*. Can't even get
published."

Colin is upset. I look at him in the half-lit gloom but fail to
bridge the gap between us. But when I ask about David Boswell,
a wonderful Vancouver comic book artist and no apprentice,
Colin looks at me. "Oh, he's been out of comic books for a long
time because he can't support his family."

And at that moment the fragility of Colin's life comes into
focus. The shabbiness of his room, which a minute ago I had
hardly noticed, becomes visible.

"Do you have Boswell's comics?" I ask.

"Of course."

"Can I see them?"

"O-kay." His voice is shy and constrained.

Colin goes into his bedroom, comes back with the books and
spreads them out before me.

Reid Fleming, World's Toughest Milkman: this character is

Boswell's great invention and the running title for his books. Much of my life appears in those books. I read them all through the years I worked in the downtown postal plant, and flipping through them now I remember the shy, downcast people I worked with. One day in McLeod's Books, breaking one of my rules, I bought one of the Reid Fleming buttons that were for sale. It showed Reid with a cigarette in his hard mouth and with his milkman bow tie on, and it carried the words, "I thought I told you to *shut up!*"

"They're great comics."

Colin slowly smiles. "I rather like Lena Toast."

So do I. I open a book and watched Reid happily gun his milk truck. Colin's own books are spread out over the floor along with comics from Germany and Japan. An exotic mix. And once again I feel the glow of fandom we experienced in Golden Age.

But it's more than that. Looking at Colin's little photocopied books with their careful figures and blocky, handprinted titles, I can almost smell the mixture of enthusiasm and desperation that led to their production. And all at once I have an image of Colin as a kind of small creature crawling on the edge of a huge golden sphere in the middle of which Paradise floats, trying to get inside.

That fall Colin lets me in on a secret. I'm sitting in his living room drinking tea when he brings out a big three-ring binder.

"You want to see the new stuff I've been doing?"

"Okay."

I leaf through the binder. He watches nervously. "I'm fairly happy with it. It's a long story. Not autobiography."

The binder contains the first three books of a projected epic called *Buddha on the Road.* "It'll contain twelve books," Colin says.

Twelve books!

The story is complicated. It revolves around Norman, an

angry soldier who's just come back to Vancouver after fighting in Bosnia for the Canadian peacekeepers. He has made a pact with a friend's dying dad to kill both the dad and God (the dad hates God, and has seen a similar streak of blasphemy in Norman). Because of this he gets picked up by a gang of tramps who drag him into Saint Anthony's church downtown to enlist him on the side of the angels.

But the tramps disgust him—he fights back. And as he fights, demons rise out of the ground to help him and also to enlist him on *their* side in their war against heaven. Norman gets dragged off by these demons, gives them advice on warfare which they applaud but don't listen to, and gets swept up in an orgy which along with the gang of tramps is easily the most cinematic thing I've seen by Colin. (But in a strange way: his dark creatures, filling their panels to bursting, seem static, frozen, like the swarming bodies on the alterpieces of a medieval church.)

What do I think as I go through the binder? Three things: the books are odd, original; they're weighty; and they're failures.

Later I think that more than anything else they are the work of an outsider. As I read them for a second time at home I can see Colin drawing in his cramped apartment while across the city the rain falls and falls. With their heavy sermonizing about the evils of religion, they have the true eccentric stink; and I can guess how well they'll sell. True, Colin includes naked women with full thighs, demons with dinosaur tails and long cocks, battle scenes and that ratlike swarm of tramps; and all this is good. But as I've seen in Golden Age, even though hundreds of new comics are out, 98 percent of them are just variations on the same thing—and *Buddha on the Road* isn't that thing. It's eccentric; and it's the work of a moralist. It's complicated in what it presents, and it shows an individual vision.

A week or so later Colin tells me that Fantagraphics in Seattle has signed on to publish at least the first three issues of *Buddha*.

"Good news eh?" he says shyly.

"It is."

"I feel a lot calmer."

"I'll bet you do."

"Who knows. Maybe this will make my name."

"Colin, I hope so."

By Christmas I own quite a few of Colin's comics. As the winter passes I sometimes leaf through them. More often, I just think about them. And each time I do I imagine a head opening up and a planet spilling out.

It's an odd planet: it contains cricket bats and scenes from the Battle of Stalingrad, tanks, Italian monks, little kids, gay men who want to be punched in the stomach. There's something of the medieval fair about Colin's imagination, something Erasmian. Like the manuscripts of a devout churchman, his drawings contain small jokes. He likes the ignorant and the wayward. And he loves specifics: a Sikh man wearing a vest, a bright-eyed young woman in a black bustier. I can imagine that kid at the bus stop appearing in one of Colin's books—for both of them, comics have been a route to the larger world.

And then, more than a year after our first talk, it's spring again and we're together in his place and Colin is floating on comics, a mild-eyed traveller on an Amazon of skinny books. Comic books spill off our laps and pile up by our feet. We talk about Herge, *Mad* magazine, the Japanese style of drawing. A cool spring wind smelling of rain blows in the open window.

Responding to a question I've just asked, Colin explains the demons in his new books. And for the first time since I've met him, he talks quickly, telling me about his father, his mother, his growing up and the terrible self-hatred that sometimes possesses him. He talks about the Vietnam War and the way it made courage and manliness—the martial virtues—suspect to his fem-

227

inist-influenced generation; and he speaks of the compression of history and how people sometimes seem to him like mousefolk now, one generation tumbling into the world on top of the next.

Then gradually the talk subsides.

"You want to read some more comics?" Colin says.

"That's an excellent idea."

He brings them out. We start to go through them. And as I enter the books, I feel sliding around me an old, old pleasure that goes back to when I was an eight-year-old in Hinton. After school I'd walk down a gravel street to Doctor Tak's dental office and sit in the chair by the table that had the pile of comics on it. And from four to five-thirty in the afternoon I'd read them through. *Little Dot. Donald Duck. The Two Gun Kid.* Sitting in Colin's cave I remember how I felt when a new comic lay on the pile—a new *Casper* or *Superman*, maybe, the glossy image on the cover promising almost unbearable excitement. I remember my little self sitting in that chair bent over the comics eating my black babies and four-cent cinnamon bun from the bakery, not speaking to the assistant, who would gently shoo me out when the office closed.

In a moment of exaltation once, Alistair said to me: "Most of us read comics when we're kids. Then we stop. Maybe flip through a *Betty and Veronica* in the checkout line at Safeway. But just try," he added, smiling with me at his elevated mood, "can you remember the ecstacy of turning those newspapery pages with their yellow and licorice colours, their little figures with their big paw hands and round heads?"

Colin remembers. He keeps visiting that world in the air we all once visited. And he isn't wrong in this. Nor is he wrong in his work. Because what could be wrong about wanting to make for others what once thrilled you and thrills you still? In fact, anything else would be a compromise.

But that's easy to say. Sitting in the spring light that fills his apartment, I watch as he carefully lifts Walrus out of the sock drawer. And I think: What does it mean to be willing to spend your life making comics—to spend that much? The question hangs in the air. But, remembering Alistair, I don't ask it. I knew by now that whatever happens in Colin's life isn't quite his decision. The page that he draws, with its panels and little figures, is his decision.

8. Joe's Beach

I

In June of 1993 I was driving down Commercial after being away on my first trip into the Interior in twenty years; and after the bright light on the other side of the mountains I noticed the street's darkness or greyness: the blackness in the heavy leaves. the dirty sidewalks, the patched pavement, the rain-blackened wood and brick walls. Everything I saw seemed both familiar and unfamiliar—exotic: an overturned Safeway shopping cart in the street, a gang of turbaned boys drinking slurpies outside the Food Stop at Commercial and Venables.

Then I saw something new. All over the store walls graffiti were spraypainted that were like nothing I could remember. Had they always been here? The commands—because they were commands—shouted at me: NICARAGUA LIBRE; SMASH CAPITALISM; SOD THE RICH; $HELL OUT; SMASH PATRIARCHY; KILL YOUR RAPIST; TAKE BACK THE NIGHT.

Their letters were big, some almost two feet high. Unlike the few pieces of graffiti I'd seen in the Interior, they had nothing furtive about them. They contained no swear words, no people's names. They weren't personal.

The graffiti addressed itself to the public at large. Yet as I drove down lower Commercial, noticing mostly Chinese shoppers, it struck me that none of these spraypainted commands had much at all to do with the neighbourhood. Most graffiti looks ugly to me, and this was no exception; but there was something disembodied about these phrases.

Back in my apartment I opened the glass patio door wide to let the staleness out. I made a cup of coffee, then sat at the kitchen counter reading my mail and looking out at the patio.

I had forgotten how dark my place was. The carpet was matted. The patio windows looked out on an alley and an abandoned car. The letdown—almost the grief—that overcomes me whenever I return home after being away for a while settled in. I listened to the Skytrain go past. Then I became too anxious to sit. I wanted to see Sharon.

Hoping to shake my mood and reconnect with the city, I took the bus downtown. And for a few minutes, before the old familiarity took over, the riders and aisles seemed grim. I noticed the hard plastic seats, meant to be knifeproof. Letters had been scratched with a pin or a very sharp knife right into the glass of the bus window. They read: JAMIE.

As we travelled down Hastings I listened to a couple talking behind me.

"Yeah he's a cunt."

"He's a fucking fag eh."

"He stole my shirt. What a cunt. He's a stealer. You should see his room, what a pigsty."

"Like he's a guy—fuck him, that's what I say."

"Somebody ought to fucking shoot him."

"Fucking slash him up eh."

"Ha ha ha! That's it! Slash up that pretty face."

As I got off the bus I turned to look at the two. They looked at me then looked away. Both of them were about fifteen, the boy with a small face and frightened eyes, the girl neat and thin-lipped.

At Hastings and Main the city looked like Lagos. A man ten yards away from me fell to the sidewalk. Then another. Then a gaunt young man in the intersection who'd bent to tie a shoelace collapsed as bonelessly as if he was a marionette whose strings had been cut. Some invisible disease was advancing down the street.

The man in the intersection got up and walked toward me. I could see he was sick. His reddish hair hung from a high-crowned cap that was too big for his head. His cheeks were scabbed and a string of dark blood hung from his nose. He came close, so close I could see his sick, wet, light-pained, remote eyes.

He pointed to the camera in my hand. "You wanna take my picture?" He grinned; his two upper front teeth were missing.

"Sure."

I focused and pressed the button.

"Can you tie my shoelace?"

I knelt and did it up. The shoelace was brown, with a number of small knots in it. The big toe had pushed through the front of the shoe.

Sharon was working in the Carnegie Centre across the street. It was volunteer work she'd taken up while I was away. "To help fill the time," she had told me on the phone.

I asked for her at the front desk. The woman—a cheerful young Native with bangs and a broad face—told she was upstairs.

I was surprised at the elegance of the wide curving stairs, the elegance of the Carnegie's stained glass windows. Plants grew on ledges. Someone had attached a handwritten sign to a nearly dead one: DON'T WATER THIS PLANT.

Sharon was working near a computer that had a screensaver that said BRIAN'S BRAIN. She looked up.

"You're back!"

"I am."

We hugged and kissed; and, holding my hand, Sharon introduced me to her fellow workers. Then we went downstairs. Sharon said, "Now I want you to meet Marie."

This was the woman at the front desk. She smiled and shook my hand and told me she had come down a year earlier from Prince Rupert. She said she felt lucky to have landed the job. "And you're lucky to have Sharon. She's goddamn great."

She and Sharon showed me around. But I was distracted. In the Carnegie Centre's small library—filled with old men who were bent over reading newspapers—I had found a revolving rack that contained nothing but Westerns.

I asked Marie, "Who reads these?"

"What's that?"

"Who reads these Westerns?"

"Oh, those. Yeah, the people here, you know. The Indians eh. The old men they like those cowboy stories."

"There's lots of Natives come here?"

"Well you know what they say. Right here at Main and Hastings is the biggest Indian tribe in Canada."

Sharon said, "Someone told me there's 10,000 Natives living in the downtown Eastside. That seems like way too many. But there's a lot."

We went outside. At the bottom of the steps leading up to the Carnegie another man fell, a tall man wearing a black cowboy hat. Two people helped him up. We sat down on the steps. An old man with wet eyes sitting next to us held out a nurse novel. People were sitting shoulder to shoulder. Sharon said, "The reason there's so many people is it's Cheque Day."

A hundred or so people slowly milled around on the corner. They talked excitedly and laughed. Drugs were openly bought. Young and not-so-young women paraded back and forth, swaying their hips, snapping their fingers in the air.

Compared to this world, compared to the garish paintings on Hastings, the graffiti back on Commercial Drive seemed almost amusing. As I walked up Sixth to my apartment I thought: Contrast SMASH PATRIARCHY with HEROIN KILLS and you can see the phantasmagoria produced by a university education and a belief in theory. This was the phantasmagoria Colin battled with, a giant tied down by it but unwilling to break the knots.

Over the next few months I discovered that the glamour of this graffiti had given it a tourist attraction appeal. People in white clothes came over from Kitsilano; and as they strolled up the street on their way to make an evening of it in Santos' or The Latin Quarter, they would look at the words—KILL YOUR RAPIST, say, or IN CASE OF EMERGENCY DIAL AK-47—and smile. One freezing January night when I was shopping at the Sunset Market I saw a drunk woman in a long leather coat put her arm around her companion and shout "Right on!" as he smashed the sole of his shoe against one of the spray-painted *Globe and Mail* boxes.

That kick made sense. The street provided a perfect stage set for romantic brutalism. As I walked I saw a dog squatting on the sidewalk having a bowel movement, a boy of about twelve who spat into the street and proudly muttered to his girlfriend, "I just spent six hours in a holding tank," a couple of South American immigrant men who stood in a doorway smoking cigarettes and looked alternately threatening and self-conscious, a man poking through a garbage can, a crippled old couple, a disturbed single woman wearing a cloth coat that was too short in the arms. I saw a beautiful girl in a hugely oversized motorcycle jacket kiss a boy who had hair in his face and a coat down to his ankles; they were right by the KILL YOUR RAPIST graffito and coming up behind them, pushing a Safeway cart full of their stuff, were two Native men, their faces pockmarked, their eyes wet and out of focus; behind *them* walked a teenage girl in hot pants and sheer stockings and high heels, slipping on the dirty ice of the sidewalk, but still determinedly pushing the baby carriage in which her new kid slept, out to have fun.

By now the area had made the papers. News stories were written about it; human interest pieces appeared in the weekend supplements. Writers in *The Globe* and *The Vancouver Sun* saw in the "cultural workers" of the Drive a rebirth of the hippie movement. The glamour that both oppressed and fascinated Colin had caught their eye. I began to cut out articles, looking for insights into what had happened.

But though I read each story with interest, I felt that they only hinted at the strange way in which the world I had known with Alistair and the Adanac gang had returned to the Drive.

One brilliant spring Saturday I met the writer Grant Buday in the Pofi bar; and with a tape recorder on the table between us and a student with dreadlocked hair holding his face in his hands one table over, we talked about the neighbourhood. We spoke about the Polish gangs of the fifties and the Indonesian women Buday had seen painting miniature totem poles in the back of a Chinese grocery store on Victoria Drive. We talked about the members of the old Clark Park gang who'd walked around in tee shirts and jeans even in the middle of winter. And becoming enthusiastic, we described to each other the skinny Vietnamese with their black clothes and black cowboy boots who played pool up at the Grandview at Commercial and Broadway.

And then, irresistibly, our talk turned to the Drive's political culture. Leaning forward, talking quickly and softly, Buday at first made me laugh.

"You've seen them?" he said. "These kids in their Moslem hats and Li'l Abner boots?"

I nodded, smiling.

"Well I've lived in the area for twelve years now. And I feel like an outsider. I do. I mean the thing is they frighten me. They have this flat look that brushes across you as if to say, 'You don't exist. You're not even here.' A killer would show more interest. I see them coming down the sidewalk and I run. I hide! I go up a side street to avoid having to encounter them! And they have that language, that political speech. And that's the language that counts. And I don't speak it. And so I'm marginalized. I'm pushed out. And I can't speak to it. They talk in front of you and every word outlines your shape. You can see what you represent to them."

I said, "And you don't like the image of yourself that's reflected back?"

He shook his head and looked out at the sunlit street. "No. It's more that they have the power and you don't. They're young and they have that youthful ignorance and confidence that I had at their age to just be cavalier about things. And they swing power here—certainly in the realm of the street. You just realize you're not really a player in all this."

When I left Buday half an hour later a sudden rain began that wet my glasses so that everything had a smashed-up look. I walked up the street. By the bank machines at First and Commercial, with my glasses now smeared from being wiped on my shirt, I saw a student (or what seemed to be a student) holding out copies of *The Workers' Vanguard.* All around him stood people lined up in the pouring rain to get money. Dressed in a wet army jacket, the student smiled at me. I smiled back but held up a hand in refusal.

Nobody else was taking the paper either. Through my blurred glasses I saw it had a wet streak down the front. The streak was shaped like a crow's wing. And seeing that, I felt a powerful deja vu: I had seen this student before, his newspaper, the people lined up in the wet and dark, even the blotches in the stuccoed

236

wall and the dimes of gum on the sidewalk. Like a photograph taken with a telephoto lens of a suburban street in which all the houses appear close up, on one plane, the years I had spent on Commercial Drive appeared before me in foreshortened perspective. And I thought: The fantasy of militant activism is still being passed on from one generation to the next.

I had first encountered that fantasy during the decade and a half I worked in the downtown postal plant. A different setting, but it was the same there too—nobody read the paper that the activists put out. *The Postal Worker* would appear, people would leaf through it then let it drop; and by the end of the night drifts of unread newsprint would litter the floor near the order books where the papers were piled.

I walked on, remembering. After a while the rain stopped. Faint shadows appeared on the sidewalk. Then the air brightened; the shadows turned black and crisp; and the sudden sun turned the wet street into a strip of blinding light. Every colour in the brick walls stood out. The sidewalk steamed. The deja vu I had had earlier returned, so that everything I was seeing and hearing seemed like something I had seen and heard before. I felt immersed in times gone by. Thinking of the *Workers' Vanguard* dealer, I remembered the intense, almost ludicrously self-alienated atmosphere that I associated with my years in CUPW. And as I walked I thought: Nothing contributes to the Commercial Drive spectacle more than this atmosphere. It seemed to be part of everyday life for many of the young people on the street, and at that moment it struck me that it was even in some ways necessary for their development as men and women.

I watched a boy and girl, both dressed in combat fatigues, get settled on the steaming sidewalk. The boy had thick black eyebrows; the girl had red hair and pale cheeks. Colin could have drawn them. I thought of the protesting kids wearing bandannas and Army jackets in one of his stories, sitting jubilantly on a tank outside the Seaforth Armoury. But hadn't I felt the same? Hadn't I gone through a period when I'd been at least as estranged from reality as these two kids? At that moment I remembered staring in fascination at Don Ross in his Huck Finn cap and black leather sportscoat; my heart caught with understanding, and I grimaced in sympathy both at my young self and the couple sitting on the sidewalk. How seemingly frivolous are the events that determine the shape of a life.

I walked on. A young woman suffused with the same narcissistic idealism that I'd known had written MY BODY, MY CHOICE on the *Province* paperbox across from the liquor store, and below that, in a painful A-student outburst, MON CORPS, MON CHOIX. And there, on that wall, a little further on—SOD THE RICH. Used this way, I thought, sod isn't even a Canadian word.

Alistair and I, both country boys, had seen Vancouver as a frontier. Twenty years later, Commercial Drive, a street we'd walked on as just one among the rest, had become another kind of frontier. Unhappy parents, mortgages, credit cards, business suits—all that was elsewhere. *This is your place,* the street whispered, and as I walked past the Paris Bakery, with the students bouncing toward me on the balls of their feet, the crowded sidewalk, the Italian and Portuguese and Jamaican shops all became part of a sort of Leonard Bernstein musical in which young people with high ideals flung open the doors of perception onto a dazzling afternoon.

II

Back home I sorted through my clippings and thought about what Buday had said. *They swing power here.* That was what my clippings said, too. In one way or another, some directly, some in passing, they all dealt with the boycott of Joe's Cafe that had taken place in 1990, an event that later became famous enough to be made into a movie. As my clippings showed, that boycott had revealed the community's heart.

By the fall of 1990, Joe's—which had then been in existence for fifteen years—had become the most fashionable coffee bar on the Drive. How this happened, the clippings suggested, was complicated.

It started with the bar's owner. A bullfighter in Portugal and then for many years a welder in Northern BC, Joe Antunes had sunk his life savings into his bar. He'd been determined to make it succeed. Yet he seemed shy and, in part because of his lack of English, oddly separate from the cafe.

This was deceptive. Soft-voiced and baby-faced he might have been; but Antunes was also an intensely stubborn man who drove a Trans-Am and admired the former dictator Antonio Salazar for making Portugal a "safe place to live." Joe had hired waiters from the old country, and he liked hanging out with the Portuguese good old boys with their big mustaches and shiny black track suits. He worked hard, seven days a week, and he wanted his place to matter to his crowd.

At the same time he was more tolerant than most of the coffee bar owners on the Drive. During the 80s, as the leftists and university students and lesbians moved in, most of the bars—The Roma, for instance, or The Pofi—had remained stand-offish. Their clientele had stayed almost entirely men, usually men of Italian background, and their decor had been both ornate and macho in the offputting European way.

It had been different in Joe's. Even after he began making money—and surprisingly for someone who so clearly wanted the respect of his Portuguese peers—Antunes had preserved the greasy spoon atmosphere of bare floors and dusty bullfighter posters that from the start had given his place its open-to-the-public flavour. Even more surprisingly, by the late 80s he was subsidizing a lesbian softball team. Very soon his bar had become known as the number one lesbian bar in the city.

Antunes was no liberal: he wasn't ideologically on the side of the lesbians at all. But he knew how his bread was buttered. And partly for that reason, partly because of his stand-back attitude his place had boomed, so much so that by the summer of 1990 the customers were spilling onto the sidewalk. As I went through my clippings, I remembered going in there one afternoon a couple of months before the boycott and encountering a wall of noise and sexual display.

The TV blared; the jukebox blared. The sun poured in. It was only four p.m. but the place was packed. Women in black teeshirts and black leather pants sat at a table along the wall; a tall skateboarder in his thirties, dressed in ripped black and with stiff orange hair, walked back and forth through the crowd slapping his board against his thigh. In the sun by the window, a young woman in a miniskirt sat on the lap of an older woman in chaps. The younger woman's lips were lush with lipstick; she held a cigarette between her fingers; she crossed her legs and showed her pubic bush.

It was as if the bar's chipped tables and pool hall chairs perfectly suited the Drive's fantasy of an environment that was simultaneously street-tough and politically correct. Antunes might have been a redneck; but he was the right kind of redneck, a softie who left you alone. As for the place itself, with its tough Portuguese atmosphere and bohemian clientele, it wasn't just a bar—it was like a soft-core fantasy of a bar.

Which was the problem. Antunes didn't see it that way. He had always been somewhat shy and stand-offish; now, as the scene in the cafe exploded, he became increasingly out of touch with his clientele. He didn't know the customers, didn't know how to talk to them; at the end he was hardly able to control what was going on.

Some lesbians I knew told me later (asking for anonymity) that by the start of the summer they had all but stopped going to Joe's. The crowd was raucous, and for many people just too coarse and overbearing to be comfortable with. Already once, Joe had had to call in the police to break up a disturbance. Then on Sunday, September 16, 1990, one of the waiters in Joe's became offended by two women who were embracing—hugging each other or kissing: reports differed as to what exactly they were up to. What was known was that the waiter reacted angrily and Joe backed him up.

The reaction was immediate. Within hours lesbians and gays in the area had called for a boycott of Joe's; within days the boycott had become a siege, with crowds of people outside the cafe, people in the street honking their car horns and small groups of protesters pulling ACT-UP tactics like pressing their bare bums against the cafe's display window. The Spike Lee movie *Do the Right Thing* had come out that summer, and activists in the city immediately began comparing the boycott of Joe's to the boycott of the pizzeria in Lee's movie. Younger militants in particular felt that Antunes needed to be hammered. Underlying everything was this idea: Joe's was *their place*; what in hell did Antunes think he was doing?

Negotiation was out of the question. Either Antunes offered a complete apology for his behavior or the boycott would continue. But a complete apology—an admittance that only he was in the wrong—Antunes refused to give. And so the two sides dug in. As the weeks turned into months, the walls of Joe's bar and the sidewalks around it became covered with slogans done in red, yellow, black and pink chalk, some of them political—SILENCE = DEATH—some of them insults directed at Antunes.

Attunes tried to explain himself. Then his attitude hardened. When the waiters who had walked out in the first week of the siege tried to come back, he refused to take them on. He started opening at five in the afternoon. Very few people came in. Certainly very few people I knew had the courage to show their faces in Joe's. Even if they sympathized with Antunes—and as the months wore on, it became hard not to—they were afraid to be considered right-wing.

Afraid. Going through my clippings, I remembered that fear. In hindsight I could see that Antunes had mishandled the situation. He was a shy man, both stiff and uncommunicative, and he had ended up running much too loose a ship for such a popular bar. Frank Murdocco and his sons at The Calabria, for instance (the current hot spot on the Drive), would never have permitted the kind of loud disorder which had characterized Joe's before the boycott. As the scene had grown in intensity, Antunes had gotten nervous, and then panicky and angry; in the end, he hadn't known how to handle what was going on—the success of his business had overwhelmed him.

But while all this was true, it was also true that Antunes had been fundamentally misperceived by his customers. His apparent softness had allowed many of his clientele to patronize him as a mellow ethnic who was as "liberal" as they felt themselves to be— a man who was "respectful" of lesbians and who ran "a totally great place," and who could therefore be bent to do whatever his customers wanted.

The bottom line was that Antunes hadn't seemed to be *hard.* He hadn't behaved like a dad, a proprietor, the way Frank Murdocco or the men who ran The Roma behaved. He was someone it seemed you could lay down the law to, someone to whom you could say, "This is *our* place—we made it, so do what we say."

So that at the heart of the Joe's story, I now saw, was fantasy—idealism, in the literal sense of the word. The series of misperceptions that had made the chain of events possible had been fuelled by idealism at every step, and when I went out that evening thinking about all this, a certain utopian idealism seemed to be central to the culture of "the Drive." This could be interesting: look at the people on the street with their shaved heads and camouflage pants, and for a moment or two you could enjoy the spectacle they presented of an anti-capitalist world where nobody grubbed for money and everyone was as liberal as a university graduate with an arts degree.

But how much this spectacle excluded! It excluded not just the Filipino or Thai immigrants lusting for a Toyota Corolla; it excluded even the basic emotions—racial pride, religious belief—that fueled the lives of most members of the community. (The largest "ethnic" group in the area was Catholic Asian.) When the boycott of Joe's was taking place, I had been stunned by how blinkered and unforgiving it was. The students who had attacked the cafe—and they were mostly students, the majority barely teenagers when Joe's had opened in 1975—had seemed at times as ferociously self-righteous as the students who had propelled the cultural revolution in China. Like children, they had thought their outrage was so valid that merely by feeling it Antunes would be swayed. They had thought nothing of insulting a man whom a month earlier they would have praised to the skies. Caught up in a fantasy orchestrated by Spike Lee, they had had no understanding of how serious their actions were. (Had Antunes been less stubborn, this business into which he had sunk his life savings might have folded.) Above all, they hadn't *seen* Antunes, hadn't recognized him for what he was, but instead had transformed an image that had been patronizing and sentimental into one that was demonic—and so had given themselves the freedom to be as hateful as they wished.

In the end the boycott was without consequence. Nothing came of it: no talks between the "militant" and "ethnic" groups in the neighbourhood. Certainly the sound and fury were great, and to their recipient they must have seemed pitiless; but once the show was over and the activists had left, Antunes was able to go on with his business.

And now the cafe was doing well. The bohemians had drifted back and there was even the occasional lesbian in the place. But the fantasy of Joe's was finished. When I stepped inside to have an ice cream and watch the six o'clock news, the bar seemed disenchanted, its atmosphere like that of a room in sober daylight after a bad argument has occurred. Narcissistic though it was, the show in Joe's had been vivid—a spectacle, a parade. Now that parade had gone by.

The man said, "You get it over there."

"Where?"

"Over there. Over there!"

I was in the Red Pepper, a joint on Commercial; and I had just learned that I had to get my own coffee from an urn. It was cold out—an arctic front had come down from the north. But the sky was brilliantly blue, and the cafe—poor, with whitewashed walls and a filthy floor but with a big front window—was filled with light.

A small crowd of young people was bunched up against the

window. In the sunlight that outlined their cigarette smoke, they seemed—bunched together like that, with their dirty old over-coats, their ripped jeans, their hugely oversized sweaters, their black runners worn over heavy wool socks—they seemed like a vision of potentiality and hope. I noticed their moments of unease (one boy had his head down, tearing his cigarette apart; a girl kept grooming her hair with her fingers and chewing on its ends). But what stood out was their delight in being together. The pleasure they took in each other was plain, and, feeling that pleas-ure, making it my own, it struck me that part of the charm of Commercial Drive lay in the fact that a similar tribal enjoyment could be seen on the street almost any time of the day.

But while it could give pleasure, this group sense, if you were in the mood for it, it could also be oppressive. I discovered this when I walked down the street in the bright cold sun.

The recently whitewashed wall of Joe's Cafe was now called "Joe's Beach"; and the reason was obvious. Now that it was sunny out (and even with the cold), men and women were lined up in chairs along the wall as if they were posing for an article in *The Face*. Black Doc Martins, ripped black jeans. Black sunglasses. Pale white skin. I saw Diane Archimbault, a delicate twenty-year-old from my building, sitting with her legs on the lap of a man in his forties. Sitting like that, Diane exuded a bland arrogance. As I passed by, she glanced at me, then looked away.

I had never sat there. And as I walked past, I felt a trace of the same excruciating self-consciousness I'd suffered when I was twelve and had just moved to Allenby. Everything about me—my thoughts, my clothes, even my bad leg—came together as a blunt sense of difference, and I remembered that white-hot flare of emotion I'd felt when every eye on the schoolground had seemed to say, *Outsider! You think we don't know you?*

Estrangement. But then estrangement was easy to feel around here, and not just on the street. Partly because of the youth cult they catered to, partly because of their invincible sense of moral superiority, no shops in Vancouver showed more intolerance than those that defined what the media knew as "Commercial Drive." Sharon had said, "They have no time for a middle aged woman. They're not interested in serving me. I fear their contempt."

I understood. Taken one by one, the elements that produced a feeling of exclusion weren't much. But when I added the display windows with their ideological art and ads for sensitive, non-smoking roommates to the unsmiling clerks who gave you a quick once-over when you walked in and measured you by your appearance to the constrained, chilly flavour of the careful conversations and even more careful stock, then the thought of how all this would make Sharon feel unsure of herself at times overpowered me.

Even more. Increasingly, I couldn't ignore the difference between the essentially civic atmosphere of downtown, where by necessity you had to accommodate a wide range of people, and the cliquish feeling of the Drive's more limited, more insular culture. How small-town the neighbourhood seemed sometimes, with its little bundle of ideas offered over and over again until they felt soiled from handling! I had stayed here too long; increasingly, the area's immense distance from the liberating anonymity of big city life choked me.

Back home I started re-reading old Roland Barthes books. I was looking for a passage. Then I found it. In a 1979 interview Barthes had said: "The historical phenomenon that seems to have been growing for ten years now is the problem of 'gregarity'—a Nietzschean word. People on the margins of society flock together, become herds, small, it's true, but herds just the same. At that point I lose interest, because conformity reigns in every herd....I just find it very difficult to put up with stereotypy, the elaboration of small collective languages, a phenomenon quite familiar to me through my work in teaching, in the student milieu....For a while, I don't dare make my escape, but finally, often because of some chance occurrence in my personal life, I find the courage to break with these languages."

All this spoke to me. Barthes' insights, yes; but even more the personal note, the sense of a crisis giving him the courage to break free. I remembered the tone of Buday's voice when we had talked about the Drive. He too had mentioned the student milieu. "There was the same thing up at Simon Fraser with the deconstruction crowd," he had told me. "It was very cliquish—and that translates down here too. And it was a matter of, 'You're just not. Quite. Getting it.' That New Age 'It.' It's a group of people who seem to be engaged in a kind of theatre piece with each other. And what you don't say is, what the unwritten text is, is, 'Don't ask me awkward questions and I won't ask you awkward questions. And we'll buy each other's facade.' Right? You have to go with the flow of the scam. And it seems to me that that's the language of Commercial Drive. It's just my trip, maybe, but I find it hard to just walk through it and laugh it off."

A small thing, that bit of conversation. But for the first time it had allowed me to see how walled-off Commercial Drive had become.

I had loved the area's complexity—its cultural complexity and its temporal complexity. I had spent my youth here, and the stucco houses still stood in which I'd lived first with Cate and then with Alistair and Ray. I'd liked the neighbourhood's living connection to the Old Country on the one hand with its family stores and delicious food, and to the traditional beer-drinking life of East Vancouver that I'd first experienced in 1970. But the atmosphere had been changed by my generation of militants and the students and bohemians who had arrived in their wake. By and large they were animated not so much by a love of the neighbourhood as by a resentment of everything that surrounded it. This resentment—so often, for the older militants, fuelled by a sense of personal failure—was a powerful force; and it had led to a garrison mentality on the Drive.

The left-wing graffiti for instance—what was it if not a kind of linguistic totem telling strangers *This is our place; watch what you say?* As with totems, there was even a sympathetic magic attached to these slogans: spraypaint NICARAGUA LIBRE on a wall and soon enough Nicaragua *would* be free; spraypaint SMASH CAPITALISM and listen to the sound of the edifice tumbling! And then there were the militants' tribal clothes and hairdos: the drab jeans, the mousy shirts, the tweed sportscoats, the cloth caps, the plain shoes, the puffy, frizzy hair pulled back in a ponytail. Like the ideas they preached, the militants' clothes strongly resisted change (change was frivolous, a sign of an interest in fashion), and because they changed so slowly they managed to accrete meaning and significance, even a sort of myth. They became "total," an expression of an ideology. You saw in them not the wink of fashion, with its love of the new and pleasurable, but something serious and unblinking. They were humourless clothes, in short, and this sense of a serious, dense, ideologically-driven kind of dress was very strong on the Drive.

But the deepest and most important manifestation of the area's walled-off mentality was an explosive anger at transgression. This anger had shown itself in a number of ways over the years. But definitely the most notable were the ideologically motivated street protests and acts of violence which had regularly punctuated Commercial Drive life. One by one they had occurred: the attempt to keep out the McDonalds on First Avenue, the torching of The Chicken Place by animal rights activists, the protest campaign mounted against the 24 Hour Video on Kitchener, the boycott of Joe's Cafe, the anonymous pamphlets attacking Circling Dawn for sexism, and, most recently, the attacks on the new Starbucks on Second.

But you didn't need to come across a protest to sense the area's anger. Week in and week out a kind of tribal resentment boiled over on the Drive. And I discovered this now. I had crept into Octopus Books to check out the magazines; and as I bent over the rack, I heard a man snarl, "What really fucking *pisses me off* is when the mainstream media calls him 'the spiritual leader of Tibet.' He is not the fucking spiritual leader. He's the leader. Period." I couldn't see him, but I could hear him, and so could everyone else in the store—in his anger he was shouting.

I thought: Would he have spoken like this in Mayfair News or any other downtown place? No. He'd have been civil; he'd have recognized that he was in a place where other people might think and feel differently than him and he'd have acted accordingly.

But this was *his* place; this was *his* part of town. And so he felt free to act as if the air that carried all our voices was just a kind of wall on which he could scrawl his anger for the rest of us to applaud.

I didn't applaud. Instead I felt suffocated, complicit some-how, as if just by standing there and doing nothing I had become part of a *fatwa* against the downtown world. It was a distasteful moment, the kind that increasingly now made the Commercial Drive area a dingy and claustrophobic place in which to live.

The next Sunday it rained. Around four o'clock, tired of being inside, I went for a walk. I headed down Commercial, then turned west. After a block I could see over the crest of the hill that descends toward the downtown Eastside. The city rose before me, as strange and flat under the sky as a photograph propped against the clouds.

The sky grew larger as the street sloped down. Coming over the rise I saw what I thought was a Vietnamese woman squatting on the bare sidewalk with her hands held over a galvanized pail containing burning wood. She watched me pass.

Then I saw something I didn't take in at first. A small child stood in front of me wearing only a black garbage bag with holes cut out for its arms and head. It was crying. It had soiled itself: excrement stained its legs and the tops of its feet. The girl—I decided it was a girl—stood in front of the open doorway of a ground floor apartment set close to the sidewalk. I could see inside; in the dark hall lay newspapers, pizza boxes, pizza crusts, ripped-open bags of garbage, meat bones, beer bottles, and over everything, swarms of flies.

I looked at all this. Then someone inside shouted, "You just stay out there, you fuck!" and the sobbing child put her hands on top of her head in a gesture of grief.

I walked on for a bit. Then I turned around.

Back on Commercial I went into the Blue Eagle Laundromat. Inside, in the warmth that smelled of hot clothes drying, I dropped a quarter into the payphone and punched a number.

The woman on the other end said: "Nine one one. How can I help you."

I explained what I had seen.

The woman said, "Okay. Did anybody hit the child? Did you see anything like that?"

"No I didn't."

"So this is not a problem for the police."

"I guess not."

"So what would you like me to do, sir."

"I don't know. That's why I called." My heart slammed in my chest. "Listen, maybe I didn't explain myself—"

"Sir, you did explain yourself. I'm just trying to find out if this is a problem for the police."

"Well, I think it is a problem for the police. That hall was filthy."

"Yes, you said that."

"And the girl was just wearing a garbage bag. Do you understand what I'm saying? She didn't have any clothes on!"

She said, "Don't shout at me, sir."

"Okay."

"Okay. Now calm down, sir. All right?"

"All right."

"Okay."

There was a moment's silence. Then she said: "All right. Now I've had a moment to think about this. I'll tell you what. I'll send a car out. Is that all right?"

I was silent.

"Is that okay?"

"Yes, that's okay."

That night I dreamt of Texas. In my dream I crossed a great desert that was almost painfully beautiful. In the distance huge clouds of yellowish dust rose up miles into the sky. I came to a town at the crossroads of two highways; the town was deserted except for a man on a horse who rode silently toward me.

When I woke the next morning I heard rain. Almost immediately I thought of the child and what I had seen behind her.

After I showered and had breakfast, I felt better. I headed out for work, walking up Sixth under acacia trees that in the rain, with their heavy leaves, cast an almost night-time blackness. On the back of the bus stop at Commercial someone had spray-painted the anarchy symbol. I decided to keep walking. Down Fifth an apartment block was being built of particle board and grey two by fours. I stepped around a half-eaten Big Mac and a crumpled-up potato chip bag. I passed a second-hand shop called Amin's and just beyond it a grocery store that I knew sold only cigarettes and pop. An anxious man, an immigrant wearing jeans that were too big for him, crossed Commercial with his elbows held close to his sides. And at Third, a few yards down the alley, a woman with long limp black hair sat on a plastic Dairyland milk crate; staring vacantly out as if she was sitting on a toilet, she pushed a needle into her arm.

9. An Assault

One night the following year, just before Christmas, I left my apartment at Sixth and Commercial to get something to eat and maybe pick up a couple of magazines. Businesses in that area ignore the holidays, and by nine p.m. most of the nearby stores were shut.

A cold night. Fog filled the air, one of those winter inversions that leaves buses coated with smoke and dirt. Under the streetlights, where the fog sifted endlessly down, I saw white frost on a pile of cigarette butts. With the fog, and with no light coming from the few store windows, Commercial Drive seemed to have travelled back in time.

Fluorescent light illuminated the lobby of Grandview Lanes—inside people were bowling and drinking coffee. Then it was dark. I could feel the fog on my face. The silence calmed me. The few people out walking looked like ghosts.

At First Avenue I got some money at the bank machine then turned back home. The fog had thickened, transforming the car lights into dim globes of incandescence. At the Star Weekly tobacco store I bought my magazines—an *Atlantic* and a *New Yorker*—which old Mubarek handed to me in a thin brown paper bag.

I walked up Commercial then crossed the street to Golden

Boys, a hole-in-the-wall where you can get a slice of pizza for a dollar. A teenage girl with thick lips and tired eyes in a painted face was shouting in Italian at the cook and at the same time talking in English on the big black phone that was on the counter.

I told her I wanted a slice with hamburger on it.

"You want it heated?"

"Just a bit. To go."

"Okay."

She did her work expertly and thoughtlessly; and when she was finished, she placed a brown paper bag in front of me with the open end neatly folded in. I paid, placed the warm bag on the palm of my hand; and, carrying the other bag between two fingers, I walked through the pizza oven warmth, pushed the door open and stepped outside.

The cold bit at me. I zipped my jacket up to my throat. Crossing the street, I noticed two Native teenage boys standing in the fog in front of the galvanized metal wall of Coastal Storage. And as I stepped onto the sidewalk, one of them walked up to me and punched me with all his force on the left side of my head, just above the ear.

The other boy immediately ran away. My head stung where I had been hit, but more than anything else I felt a gaping surprise.

I said, "What the hell is with you?"

The boy came toward me, his face congested with rage. He said, "You fucking pom!" and then he punched me again in the same spot above the ear.

I was stunned; I shouted, "What the fuck is wrong with you!"—still thinking I could respond like that, that words would make a difference—but again he came at me and again punched me in the same place.

Intense pain, intimate and local. My glasses fell to the ground. And now adrenalin poured through me. It was the glasses dropping: I suddenly realized I was being attacked and that I could get hurt. The boy hesitated, as if seeing the change in me. I screamed something at him. I dropped my parcels. I grabbed his arms; I pushed at him, still shouting, pushed as hard as I could, trying to stop him; and at that moment, as if in a TV show, a police car swerved up onto the sidewalk beside us. Within seconds the two officers had separated us and the boy was in handcuffs.

It had all taken place in about a minute. But it started to upset me almost at once. At first I felt gratitude, and amazement that the police had arrived so quickly. But as I stood there on the sidewalk telling the officer I was okay and trying to fit back a lens that had popped out of my glasses, I found I was speaking in a false tone of voice—I was trying to assert myself in front of this policewoman.

I felt ashamed of what had happened. I saw myself as the police saw me—a short, flustered, middle-aged man who had been punched in the side of the head and whose glasses had been knocked off.

Another police car pulled up onto the sidewalk. When the policewoman went to talk to the new arrivals, I realized my temple and jaw were throbbing with pain.

The woman returned and said, "There was a similar assault about twenty minutes ago just a couple of blocks away. It looks like this is the one who did it." She glanced at the boy, then back at me. "He's had a busy night, wouldn't you say?"

"I guess he has."

"So will you lay charges?"

The handcuffed boy was backed up against the wall of Coastal Storage, about four yards from us. The car lights shone on him. He was drunk; his face was blank. I said, "Oh, Christ, I don't know. He's just a kid," and in my voice I heard sentimentality and officiousness. "…I mean, something's clearly bothering him....That's got to be looked at....Putting him in jail, I don't see how that could help...."

The officer stared at me. "I can tell you, we're not going to put him in leg irons or anything like that. He'll spend the night in juvenile detention and hopefully dry out."

She paused. "Sir, he assaulted you. From what you've said, he punched you in the head a number of times for no reason. I can't tell you what to do. But if you don't press charges we have to let him go."

That startled me. I thought of someone else going through this. I looked at the boy. And slowly indecision left me. "Okay, I'll lay charges," I said. But as soon as the words were out I felt harsh and vindictive.

In the back of the police car I wrote out the particulars. The officer had an accent, and when she read the word "pom" she said in her light dry voice, "That's odd. Where I come from that means "limey" or "Brit." You sure that's what he said."

"That's what I heard."

"Well—"

She explained to me the subpoena that would be sent, told me that I would have to show up in court. Then I was free to go.

Back in my apartment I started to feel anxious. As the night passed my anxiety grew. I couldn't read. I couldn't look at the *VR* pages I had to edit that week. I sat at the kitchen counter, rigid with concentration. Why me? Was it my face? Something in my walk or attitude? What had I done to bring this on? In sudden flurries of emotion I saw an insipid weakness in myself, something hateful in my expression.

But this was stupid! And then another feeling: a choking rage. I should have KICKED HIM; I should have SMASHED HIS FACE. I wallowed in images of violence, my mouth and jaw set in a rictus of anger. Adrenalin pumped through me. Then the images died out; anxiety seeped back. I read. I struggled with my thoughts. Two or three hours passed. Finally I felt exhausted and went to bed.

Over the next couple of days the fog left and was replaced by freezing rain. Christmas was upon us. The area around Sixth and Commercial is a poor one, and during Christmas the suffering people undergo there is intense. I was burdened with my own Christmas concerns, but what had happened had shaken me up and made me more than normally sensitive to the outside world. Everywhere I looked I saw pain and grief. Staring from the bus window on my way to work one day, I watched a Chinese woman walk up Commercial with slow, indecisive steps. She was young, dressed in a cloth coat; her face was contorted with anguish.

And the bus itself seemed horrible. Each day it was packed with poor people going downtown, worried, badly dressed people who pressed together in a suffocating manner. I imagined the Tylenol 3s, the tubes of white toothache cream for their bad teeth, the way some of them would get drunk early in the day, celebrate, then emotionally scrape the bottom of the barrel, so that by four in the afternoon they would have nothing more to give, either to their kids or each other. I hated the heavy, coarse-faced men who postured like schoolyard bullies in the middle of the aisle, and could hardly stand to look at some of the other men—unbearably anxious forty-year-olds in tee shirts and jeans who kept adjusting their baseball caps. There were mothers who spoke to their kids with the dead, self-pitying voices of women who were never listened to, and other mothers who wrung their hands over and over again, squeezing the soft part of their palms, looking out the bus windows with eyes wet with worry.

Worst of all was the change in myself. One afternoon at work I tried to describe it to Jules Marchand. Jules, the former Calgary man whom Gunther and I had worked with back in the plant, had become a driver. Now we were working together on

K's dock. Jules handed lettertainers to me from the back of his truck and I stacked them on the dock, working quickly, the bottom of each lettertainer snapping into the top of the one below. A cold wind blew down the alley; the stink of diesel and gasoline from the idling trucks filled my nose. I said, "I've never felt this before. If I see some guy walking toward me, I can just feel my walk getting aggressive. And I think, 'Boy, if he so much as touches me, man, that's it!'"

Jules looked at me. "You never felt that before?"

"I haven't ever."

He shook his head.

"And you know what?" I said. "For the first time in my life I want to wear things like steel-toed boots and leather jackets. I don't walk with my hands in my pockets any more. I carry my umbrella like it was a club."

This was true. I was acting like a bully, learning for myself what was meant by the old cliche that violence breeds violence. Walking to my bus stop in the dark I felt raw and mean. At odd moments I would be seized by an anger so ferocious it left me shaken. I noticed the brutality of men's faces in my neighbourhood, saw the passivity in their wives or girlfriends, the cringe in their kids, or else the imitative bullying. A week or so after my assault I watched a family group on the sidewalk at Hastings and Templeton—the man a Native with long hair, the woman white, the kid a boy of about five. It happened in front of me. The boy rushed toward the man, excited by something; the man, his face ugly with sudden rage, raised his arm as if to hit the boy; and the boy instantly cringed away. I noticed two things: that the boy was used to this, and that the woman was complacent, cowed, clinging to the man's arm even as he raised his fist.

Choking anger: I watched, I observed it all; I did nothing.

Weeks passed. I wasn't called to court. Instead a social worker phoned me up one day in January to tell me that the boy who had assaulted me was writing me a letter of apology, a letter that he hoped I would accept.

The social worker had a young teacher's or salesperson's voice, full of unctuous enthusiasm. He said, "The boy is basically a very good kid. And he's truly sorry. And I think, you know, what he did was pretty minor, so I'm really hoping—"

"It wasn't that minor," I interrupted. "He punched me in the head three times."

There was a pause. "Oh, I didn't know that."

"You didn't know that?"

"No, I wasn't informed of what he had actually done."

I was silent for a moment; then I said, "Well—that's too bad, you know."

Another short pause. Then I said, "Well, sure, send the letter. I'll accept it. That's fine. Okay?"

The letter came about a week later. It was printed in pencil in big letters on a lined sheet of paper. It said, "DEAR MR SERAFIN, I AM VERY SORY FOR WHAT I DID. I DID NOT MEN IT WHAT I DID AND I FEEL BAD ABOUT IT. I AM BETTER NOW. I DID NOT KNOW WAT I DID SO I AM SORRY TO ALL THE PEOPLE I HURT. I APOLIGIZE TO YOU FOR WHAT I DID. I HOPE YOU ACCEP MY APOLIGY. YOURS TRULY," and then there was the boy's signature.

The letter bothered me. It was unsatisfying; it wasn't the same as a day in court. At the same time, with its misspellings and its tight, laboured-over signature, I found something intimate and hard to bear in the message the boy had put together. I kept it around for a while; then I put it away in a drawer.

One morning not long afterward I was on the Victoria bus near Main and Hastings, stopped by an impassable jam of traffic. I looked out the window. A cold grey day. A few snowflakes were falling. On the wide sidewalk by the Carnegie Centre I noticed what seemed like a river of people walking on crutches. Damaged men and women stood everywhere, people walking with the slow, timid, small-stepped, hesitant walk of the sick. I saw people hug each other, put their arms around each others' shoulders.

On the bus a man and woman started arguing. Both of them wore high-crowned baseball caps. The caps made them look countryish. The man began to talk loudly, showing teeth that had gaps in them and were black in places with decay. It seemed they were trying to find the woman's auntie. The woman was drunk. Gesturing vaguely at the window, she said, "She's just over there, fucking Christ."

The man, too shy to walk down the aisle to the driver and speak to him as an equal, called out: "Sir, d'you think you could let us off, please?"

His voice. It was whining, obsequious, in the way of poor people addressing those who are better-off. And I thought: How many years I've had to listen to this voice! I had first heard it when I'd returned to Vancouver from Texas; and I was hearing it still. It came from that old world of Powell and Hastings and Alexandra Streets that it sometimes seems to me I might never be able to leave.

The driver with visible contempt opened the door. As they stepped off the bus I wiped away the mist that had started to fog the window and leaned closer in to watch them. The snow was falling harder. The man pointed down the sidewalk: "Come on. *This way!*" Then he walked off. But she stayed, leaning against a wall, full of unhappiness. She wore a short white coat made with fake fur and had pencil-thin legs in dirty white tights that barely covered her bum.

Then I recognized her. It was Ruth Price, the woman I had sorted beside all those years before in the plant. How terribly the years had dealt with her. She had been solidly built, with good hips; now she looked shrunken. For a moment her gaze caught mine; it seemed she didn't recognize me.

The man took a few steps down the sidewalk. Then he stopped. As I watched, he turned back toward Ruth and they looked at each other, grief in both their eyes. Then he put his arm around her, murmured to her, and they walked off together.

I watched them go. They walked down the sidewalk in the falling snow. I saw: water running down the sidewalk, cripples, native Indians, skinny women with big stomachs, the horrible cold hell of video games and porno movies next to the Roosevelt Hotel.

10. *Ilira*

After I came back to Vancouver—for years afterward—I didn't buy many BC books. Maybe four at the most. I saw no reason to get more. Whenever I thought about even the books I had bought I always came up with the same set of pictures. They were crude. They reminded me of the pictures on the cards you used to find in packs of cigarettes. I could detach them easily from their stories, which were about men sitting in beer parlours who spoke the English of green chains and linecutting camps.

Reading, you'd see one of these men bend forward and lick the glued edge of the Vogue cigarette paper that he had rolled around some tobacco. He'd have worked the tobacco with his fingers as he rolled the paper around it. And now he'd move his beery tongue across the strip of glue, holding the rollie in the thumbs and first two fingers of his hands. If the writer was ambitious, you'd learn that the man's fingers were stained right up to the knuckles from the cigarettes he smoked.

The writers who wrote about these men—many of them writers I'd met in the Odlum Drive house—knew that the world they were trying to describe was completely different from the worlds they had absorbed in books. They lived in a province larger than most countries, and at its southwestern tip was

Vancouver, a cold jungle port of wooden buildings that was part Chinese, part British, part Native. Even here, even this far south, where the monkey trees grew in the West End, when the wind brought rain out of Dollarton you thought you could smell spruce and muskeg.

It was hard for a writer to avoid being picturesque. It was hard to see past the surface. You just had to walk into the Egmont or the Blackstone to recognize the truth of the saying that all BC culture flowed out of a beer bottle. I'd come back from Houston in 1970; but even ten years later, the ebbing and rising surf of noise in the smoky hotel basements remained potent and strange. Whenever I pushed through a pub's doors and sat with the loggers and the old Indians who had cowboyed in the Chilcotin or worked a skidder up near Louis Creek I knew I was going to get involved in drinking in a way that never happened in Texas.

The pubs were living rooms. And emergency wards. They smelled of damage. The men who drank in them drank until they lost the use of nouns. They lived in an hallucinatory, cramped, womanless world where even though their pants were wet with piss the waiters kept banging glasses of beer onto the sopping table, and when they spoke, or tried to, their livid memories of chainsaw accidents and the Second World War grew more broken up with each mumbled phrase.

Their world wasn't like Toronto. They were stunted men. And when they told stories it was easy to see them as a set of pictures on cards. Their narratives lacked perspective. They lacked a sense of BC as anything other than a place of hallucination, and the terrible violence in their stories was a symptom of that fact.

With a few exceptions the written stories about this milieu that I read in the Odlum Drive house and afterward weren't very good. The writers romanticized. Their sense of history was makeshift. Their models came from the US and didn't fit well. Above all they had little inner freedom or distance on what they were writing about. They produced simplified characters and wrote in an awkward style that parodied street talk. Exceptions were pressed on me, usually older books—I remember Gene telling me I should read *Hetty Dorval*. But they seemed to me genteel. The rawness—the thing I'd felt all around me the first time I walked up to the Egmont after I returned to Vancouver and smelled the beer out on the sidewalk and inside heard a wall of noise that seemed somehow redolent of the "northern" world of old wooden buildings out on the street—that rawness was missing.

Then in 1982, six years after I started working in the downtown postal plant, I read a book of another kind, a non-fiction book, Hugh Brody's *Maps and Dreams*. The book's structure was complicated; parts of it were opaque. But I was overwhelmed by it. After that I read all of Brody's books I could find: *Indians on Skid Row, The People's Land, Living Arctic.*

They were brilliant works, written with a precision and freedom lacking in the fiction I'd read. Brody, a British emigrant, wrote about the Inuit and Indian cultures of Canada. He treated these cultures seriously. He presented the inhabitants of these cultures as human beings whose apparent strangeness could be understood if you were willing to give yourself up to a world that seemed different than your own.

When I followed Brody exploring why Indians on Skid Row fought and drank, why adolescent Inuit had such desperate love affairs, why Natives coming into town off reserve sometimes hung out together in weedy lots where nobody else went, I was dazzled by the light Brody's writing shone on a subject that had been in front of me all my life but that the stereotypes I'd grown up with had kept me from understanding.

And Brody made me see how similar I was to the Natives.

Reading him I experienced constant shocks of illumination. How much I was like this! The anxieties of the Indians, the uncertainty they felt in well-lit supermarkets—I could see myself. Hadn't I—moving again and again as a boy across Western Canada and the US, feeling out of place and in my late teens so morose because of my acne that I'd lurked at home like a restlessly sick phantom, waiting for my girlfriend to write or call—hadn't I known barren and destructive love affairs just like those Inuit boys had? Hadn't I grown up with the same inhibitions, the same inability to speak out freely or even to look into my interlocutor's face?

In Brody's *Indians on Skid Row*, in particular, I found the best description I had ever read of the hippie environment I'd lived in when I returned to Vancouver. With Brody's help—and reading him, it seemed so clear—I saw that the excitement that in Texas had lain in the convulsed social order—the friends who had gone underground, the other friends who'd come back from Vietnam and spoken nervously of what they'd seen—I saw that this excitement in Vancouver had lain in the drinking itself: in beer and music and romantic love and the exaltation of men down from the bush spending their cheques. The Vancouver hippies were on unemployment insurance and welfare; and they accepted that. They accepted that their world was regulated by the government, that they were clients of the government, part of a client culture. They were dependents, like the Natives in Brody's books. And reading Brody I came to see what I hadn't seen before, that with a few exceptions the Canadian hippies had felt no one could achieve anything substantial, no one could start anything. What went on in the pubs was a spree culture, jukebox music and love affairs (the obsessive love affairs of young people with nothing to do) joining with the beer and the marijuana and hashish that permeated the scene. It was a bacchanalia, really—it was ecstatic and also damaging, and though the ecstasy in the

265

beer parlours had connected me to Native culture and later seemed to me to be the most important stratum of my experience of Vancouver, that ecstasy so warped my vision that only when my best friend died in a car crash after a night drinking did I start to see clearly again.

Reading Brody, the years I had spent in Vancouver fell into a pattern. I was amazed to see this pattern. I felt that in Native culture Brody had found the emotional core of my life. Reading him, I saw my place in the world, Western Canada, in a new way. Colonized, made deeply insecure by its swamping by an outside culture, in Brody's books I found a client society whose most authentic expression of itself was an all but speechless communion with the bush. More then once as I read I thought of the Americans who had come to Revelstoke Park when I was working there. How well-equipped and careful of themselves they'd been compared to the Canadians, Native and white, who'd driven up with cases of beer and at most a plastic tarp and stayed up drinking and staring at the bush around them while the Americans slept in their tents.

A few years later I listened to my mom lay out a history of dispersal and change. I started the *VR*. And then one day in late April 1995, on leave from the post office, I drove into the Interior for the second time in two years.

And now I stayed for a while. I criss-crossed the Cariboo and the Thompson-Nicola; and as I drove through Merritt and Savona and 100 Mile House I felt I was entering a world that intersected the world from Jasper to Medicine Hat that had held my childhood. So to travel through it deeply affected me. Like clothes put in a box that stays unopened for years, it was saturated with that feeling you get when you finally lift a shirt out and remember wearing it.

I was especially moved when I traveled the gravel roads west of Highway 97. With an almost supernatural intensity, childhood memories of dusty car seats and open pine forests rose before me. Sometimes when the sky was white I'd see a doublewide trailer set a hundred yards into the bush; there the manager of a two-pump gas station lived with his family. And I'd feel the loneliness and sense of isolation that for me has always been part of bush culture. A satellite dish would sit under the trees; but that constant euphoria and sense of cultural connection that TV provided in Vancouver would seem absent. So that when I pulled over and stepped out into the cold air and heard only the wind in the thick black trees and the noise of the cars on the highway, the cariboo bush around me seemed so still and bleak it was as if I was on a forgotten plateau on the top of the world.

It was the camp sensation. All my life, it seemed, I had been familiar with it: the dusty cigarette smell of trucks, the plywood cafes, the railroad tracks running alongside the highway on their built-up chunk gravel beds. In camp culture nature and the man-made world met with clarity and harshness, and as I travelled I saw that clarity and harshness everywhere.

When I came back to Vancouver, waiting for me among the numerous puffy packages addressed to *The Vancouver Review* was one that contained a book by George Blicke.

George Blicke was the first writer I read who described the Interior world to me. He had written little at the time I first read him—some journalism for the old *Georgia Straight*, then three or four stories for *The Capilano Review*. But he had also written a long piece for *Northern Town*, a book about Prince George published in 1972 as part of the Caledonia Writing Series.

Two hundred copies of the book were printed. It was typeset in IBM Selectric and contained photocopied pictures of Prince George's logging trucks, buildings, mills, railroad tracks and bars.

I found a copy one day in the SFU library's Special Collections; and standing in that cramped room leafing through it, it seemed to me remarkable. The way the pictures complemented the text immediately made me want to do the same, but it was Blicke's long piece—almost 7,000 words—that most affected me. It spoke of the violence of the bars, the self-hatred of the Indians and whites who lived and died down by Prince George's railroad tracks. As I read the piece I felt a great excitement. Here was a world I knew intimately; the world —the bush world, the camp world—that I had grown up in.

And then I met the man who had written the piece.

In Revelstoke in 1973 when I was working in the park I became friends with the Mission City Boys—a steel gang that rode up and down the Canadian Pacific rail lines repairing the tracks. On Sunday we would do our clothes in the Sunny Laundrette. While our jeans sloshed in the big washers, we sat outside on the bench smoking and looking around. We had a good view: we could see Railway Avenue, the five or six shining lines of railroad tracks, bush, the TransCanada Highway, and on the other side of the highway the bulk of Revelstoke Mountain.

George Blicke was working with the Boys. We became friends; and a week or two after I met him, he gave me a copy of *Northern Town*. George was thin, tall, with a drooping German mustache, strawlike hair down to his shoulders and a brooding face. Like the rest of the Boys he wore running shoes, bell bottom jeans and a jean jacket worn over a kangaroo jacket in a style that was common then in the Interior.

The Mission City gang was tough; but they accepted George as a sort of philosopher, and I derived authority in their eyes from being his friend. Soon I had the run of the railroad.

One day the two of us deadheaded on a train to Kamloops and went to the old David Thompson Hotel to drink. There among hooting young men (the young men who still dominate Kamloops, as I was to discover years later, standing in line for a movie and watching a gang of them walk up and take their place at the front), there we watched a middle-aged stripper remove her hot pants and panties and bra on a plywood circle about five feet across that was raised a few inches above the hotel floor. No coloured lights gave her a cosmetic skin. In the raw afternoon sunshine streaming in through the dirty windows, the hair on her pudenda, thick and rising up to her stomach, and the stretch marks on that stomach were risibly clear. She lifted her sagging tits, long tits with wide brown aureoles. Fearful, weary, she shook those tits at the roaring cowboys three feet in front of her.

Seven or eight glasses of beer later and so drunk I could feel it on my skin, George and I walked in the wind and dust along the tracks beside Lake Kamloops. The dust blew into our eyes and coated our lips.

"Too bad Duck's not here," I said.

"Duck would still be in the bar."

"He'd be trying to grab that stripper's tits."

"He'd have his prick out. He'd be waving it in the air."

"He's a good guy, Duck."

"He's the best. He's the best of that bunch. He wouldn't go to Kamloops though. He calls it the asshole of BC."

I looked at the dust blowing across the railroad tracks. "Oh, I don't know. It's not so bad."

That fall, George, like me, went back to school. Like me, he enrolled in SFU's English Department. Unlike me, he became a student of Phil Woolford, one of the two gurus, as Rufus had called them, each of whose classes Rufus and Paul and I had sat in on once and then avoided.

Over time his earlier directness left him. The writing he showed me on the occasions when we met—and those occasions became fewer as the years passed—seemed laboured. He published a book of stories that showed Woolford's influence. I don't think it was reviewed. He moved to New Westminster and got a job as an instructor at Douglas College. Each time I saw him he had become a little heavier, a little more angry.

But then he published a second book. This was the book that was waiting for me in the puffy package. It was a big book, almost 300 pages long, and as soon as I saw it I became excited. I immediately started reading it; and at first I thought it was going to be all right. It started with a long anecdote of almost twenty pages about going into a restaurant in Prince Rupert, and I recognized in that anecdote the honest clarity I'd seen in his piece in *Northern Town.*

But by the second chapter I realized his new book was very bad. It was a confused analysis of the BC Interior that relied on the ideas George had learned from Woolford—for instance, that Russian communism had never had a chance to show what it could really be. Structurally the book was a mishmash; even worse, it preached and preached.

After those first twenty pages I felt bored. The most living thing in the book, I thought, was its anti-Americanism.

I understood the anti-Americanism. I felt it myself. I became ashamed when I saw street people on Hastings or Granville wearing leather jackets printed with the American flag. We were Canadians, struggling, like any colonial people, to define ourselves. But George hadn't examined his anti-Americanism. And I thought: What good is that? If you were Canadian, you had to *understand* that hatred. You had to see it as a symptom of your colonial situation; you had to explore it.

But George hadn't done that. I wrote a review of his book. I praised the directness of its opening, which made you see what was really there, and I mentioned the earlier long piece in *Northern Town*; but, I said, the book's Marxism and its unexamined anti-Americanism weakened it.

When my review came out, George called me up. He berated me. He was drunk; he shouted. Then he wrote me a hate letter. I read it when I received it, unable to stop myself, then immediately put it in the garbage, pushing it down to the bottom of the bag under the sink, down under the coffee grounds and egg shells.

I thought George's letter would be the end of my connection to him. But then in the same month that I got the letter—and feeling anxious now, full of the vision I'd had on my travels but unable to do anything with that vision, gloomy because of my experience with George, certain that I had hurt him in an irreparable way—feeling anxious, I enrolled at UBC as a PhD student. My leave from the post office, now over, had stretched to almost two years: during that time off I had finished my MA. Now I wanted to quit the PO: I wanted desperately to make a move.

My first three classes disillusioned me. I had become middle-aged, and I felt both over- and under-prepared, cut off in basic ways from the other students.

Then I enrolled in a class I thought would change that. The class—called "BC Writing: 1965-1980"—contained many texts: stories and poems by Daphne Marlatt, Gladys Hindemarch, Joy Kogawa, Paul St. Pierre, D.M. Fraser, Ethel Wilson, Audrey Thomas, Brian Fawcett, Phyllis Webb, George Bowering and others, all bound up in photocopied stacks. And it contained George Blicke's long piece from *Northern Town*.

That first day, flipping through my stack, I felt excited. Stories and poems I might have shrugged at when I first read them now blazed with romance: the romance of the past, the romance of history I had myself lived through. But then within one or two weeks it was as if I was once again sitting in on the classes of the gurus. I learned that some texts were paid attention to while others—George's among them—were left untouched. The other students' ideas and statements were permeated with critical theory, and that theory, I saw, determined who they gave their time to. What seemed to me the best writing was shrugged off. But other writing that seemed to me mediocre or worse was endlessly picked over.

I felt angry; then old and unsure of myself. Then I became frustrated. Because it was impossible, using the theories the students armed themselves with, to see the texts as having come from a particular place and time, to feel one's way into them.

In that seminar room the students unlinked themselves from the city and province in which they lived and submerged the texts they were studying in other, secondary texts. And it amazed me how in tune with each other they were. They never argued. Statements were put forward—sometimes frivolously, sometimes with a kind of toneless certainty. But the world of the stories and poems stayed unexplored.

The woman teaching the seminar showed some, though not all, of the characteristics of the gurus. So I should say something here about those men. Both were transplanted Americans, clever men with a strong sense of style, who had gotten jobs at SFU when the university opened in 1968. Both cherished themselves physically, wearing expensive clothes—heavy, shiny shoes, widewale corduroy pants in deep greens and browns, leather jackets that lay across their shoulders like bucklers. Both cultivated an unctuous style that masked the fact that they allowed no debate in their classrooms. And both—the sin that for Rufus especially condemned them—wrote little and badly: clotted prose, derivative, half-expressed ideas. For all their cleverness, Paul and Rufus and I felt they were frauds. Most of all, we felt they had a contempt for the Canadians who semester after semester came under their spell.

The professor at UBC reminded me of them in the way she cherished herself, dressing in shiny black leather. Also like them, she had an unctuous manner that masked a deep dislike of debate: more than once, smiling, she said, "I want to encourage discussion."

But she lacked their con man's falsity; she wasn't a guru after all, merely brittle and vain. Twenty years earlier, with Rufus and Paul, I would have cut her class. But now I was middle-aged: I had to succeed. And gradually I became afraid of her. She was so little connected to the course material, and at the same time so relentless in her insistence that the class be "contemporary" (texts by Spivak, Baudrillard and Foucault were the ones the class actually had to read), that after a month a kind of freezing decorum had settled in. No ideas could be advanced in this atmosphere but those already put forward by the theorists.

My unhappiness grew. As the weeks passed I started to dread not only the seminar but even going up the stairs of the Buchanan Building to the English Department. In order to pump up the funds it received the Department had allowed a huge pack of graduate students through its doors. And so a court atmosphere had developed. You could get nothing—not a degree, not even a part-time teaching assistant job—without having a professor "sponsor" you.

This meant you had to flatter to survive. And you had to flatter well: because of the sheer number of students wagging their tails you had to be not just intellectually vivacious but attractive and almost romantically intense in order to stand out. So many MA and PhD students wandered in and out of the office that we didn't even have pigeonholes for department mail—instead each person had a file folder with his name on it that had to be pulled out of a cabinet.

That cabinet. It was crammed tight with the folders, which were grubby and furred with handling. I'd bend over the cabinet and finger through the tightly packed folders to get to mine; and as I did so, other students would line up behind me: seminar sharks, teacher's pets finicky with distaste at being hemmed in, middle-aged Chinese emigre students wearing light-coloured crewneck sweaters, their glasses thick, their thinning hair combed over. We avoided each other's eyes, spoke in clipped sentences, and showed in every aspect of our behavior how desperate the competition was for jobs, scholarships and professorial favour.

And no matter how hard we tried, sometimes we'd bang into each other's shoulders. The department's office was large; but the huge Victorian counter behind which the support staff did their work cut off three quarters of it, so that to get your mail you had to bunch up with the others in a closet-wide pathway.

A humiliating situation. And then an event occurred. It was small in itself, but it tipped a balance, making me realize that what I had intermittently thought almost from my first week at UBC—that I didn't belong here and wouldn't succeed—was in fact the case.

The seminar on BC writing was over. It was raining, dark out. The overhead fluorescents glared on the hard surface of the big table. We had all been writing papers for weeks, and we were anxious and tired. My dislike of the teacher—and my fear of her, of her power—had become so great that by now I could hardly look her in the face.

That night there was little discussion. Katya Brodsky, a student from St. Petersburg whom I had talked to a few times on the bus, kept sniffling, her eyes red and her face drawn.

But the professor was festive. She wore shiny black leather pants and a tight-fitting black sweater that showed off her breasts. As we were packing up to leave, she looked at us over her narrow reading glasses, their frames also black. And she smiled: the brisk smile of a veteran chairperson.

"Now about the end-of-semester party," she said. "We live

in Shaughnessy, so I'll have to draw a map. As I'm sure you know, the streets are somewhat tangled around there." The smile again. "Now. We'll provide the wine and the main course. You can bring dessert.

"And you can bring beer if you'd like. But I would ask you to please take the bottles with you when you leave."

No beer bottles. I thought—but thought isn't right: it was an upwelling of hatred—I thought of how every one of the texts we had studied that fall was suffused with the beery light I'd first seen when I returned to Vancouver from Texas in 1970—that light on Cordova Street when you stepped, blinking, out of the Egmont into the afternoon. I saw the cases of beer bottles that were always piled up on the back porches of the houses I'd lived in; I saw Alistair wiping his mustache after drinking while keeping his right hand curled in a fist on the terrycloth table; I saw the glasses of beer with their plimsoll lines that I had drunk after his death and the people I'd drunk them with; and I saw the way the hotel beer parlours in which we had sat had made a chain of indigenous culture stretching from Nanaimo to Whitehorse.

But I said nothing. Instead I lowered my eyes and doodled in my notebook.

How powerful social structures can be. The professor smiles; I sit before her with my back bent, my head lowered, a man in his forties unable to make the quip that would ease the emotions her words provoked. Those emotions resulted (I realize now) from the class structure that ordered the room; more exactly, they were due to the experience of being put in your place, the quintessential colonial experience, which I had reacted to the way people have always reacted to such experiences, unable to salve the wound and unable to wound back.

I tried to write about this experience. But I was too close to it; my writing went nowhere. I put my notes away. Then in 2001, Hugh Brody published a book called *The Other Side of Eden.* It was a big book, a kind of culmination of his earlier books. Right near the beginning I marked a passage that dazzled me. It seemed to speak to so many things: to what I felt about myself; to what I had felt when I first came back to Vancouver from Texas; to the sense of inadequacy that then and for years afterward had seemed to me to determine Canadians' relationship with others; to the kinship I had felt with many of the people I'd met in the Interior, first in Revelstoke then on later trips; and to what I had felt in that seminar. Brody was talking to an Inuit man named Anaviapik:

> So ilira *is to do with being afraid? I asked. Like* kappia*? No, not that kind of fear. And not the* irksi *kind of fear either. Anaviapik gave examples of what might make you feel* ilira*: ghosts, domineering and unkind fathers, people who are strong but unreasonable, whites from the south. What is it that these have in common? They are people or things that have power over you and….make you vulnerable….*
>
> *The word* ilira *goes to the heart of colonial relationships, and it helps to explain the many times that Inuit, and so many other peoples, say yes when they want to say no, or say yes and then reveal, later, that they never meant it at all.*

That night, when the professor told us we could bring beer to the end-of-semester party, but would have to take the beer bottles home, I wanted to quit. For some time what I'd been doing at UBC had seemed artificial, a thing I would never get through. But like so many others who have felt this I kept my growing certainty of failure a secret even from myself.

I kept my head down. I finished my classes. I decided to go on. But then a few weeks into the next semester, when I learned I wasn't getting the TA-ship I needed to pay for my tuition, I explained to one of the department secretaries that I was a Ph.D. student and could use some support. She looked at me. In a tired voice, she said, "To be blunt, you should have gotten a professor to back you." A few days later, I left.

In Christmas of 2002, at a book launch at the Railway Club, I ran into George Blicke. He was sitting at the end of the long narrow back room, near a window. When he saw me he waved. I didn't know what to make of that. I raised my hand, and he waved me over. I walked toward him. I felt, not anger, but wariness, uncertainty.

He said, "Come on. Sit down. Let's make up."

I sat. We talked and drank beer. It seemed he had forgiven me and hoped that I had forgiven him.

The conversation turned to the past. He said, "You remember Bobby Eddie?"

"Duck?"

"Duck, yeah."

"Sure. Of course I remember him."

"He died. Just a while ago. He had a heart attack."

"Shit, that's too bad," I said. "That's too bad. Fuck."

I had sat down feeling wary and fragile. Now I felt upset. A piece of my past—invaluable, irreplaceable—was gone.

"I liked old Duck," George said.

"So did I," I said.

I drank beer. Then I said, "I remember once out past Three Valley Gap when you and me were suntanning up on one of the boxcars. Duck found that Chinese grave. Remember that?"

"I don't think I do. What happened there?"

"Well, it was this old mass grave, I guess you could call it that. It was a bunch of sticks sticking out of the ground. But Duck noticed they had Chinese lettering on them. I guess they commemorated some railroad workers. I remember how excited he got. I remember him saying, 'Shit fart Cadillac, boy, I can see those Chinese squatting here by the river ki-ying to each other.' He had that lingo."

George nodded. "Bobby was good."

We talked some more, about Bobby Eddie, about the other boys, about the old days in Revelstoke. And for a while I felt the lightness that comes with reminiscing about the past.

It didn't last. As we drank, the old emotions became overlaid with the new emotions that had grown up in their place. You can't go back to the old scenes untouched. I felt after a while a gloom, a melancholy.

And then other people I knew, people from the *VR* days, showed up. I was no longer involved with that magazine or any magazine, and I started to feel stressed or stretched, unable to keep up with the different conversations. They were other people's stories now, not mine.

I left. Outside on Dunsmuir Street it was raining. I looked up at the fine lines of rain falling in the streetlights. I had first really seen those lines of rain, had first really taken note of them, when I was twenty-two and had worn a toque and bellbottomed jeans. Looking up, I remembered that. I could feel the beer buzz on the skin of my face, and the wetness of the rain. That sensation of wetness and slight numbness took me, for real now, into the past.

A NOTE ABOUT THE AUTHOR

Bruce Serafin was born in St. Boniface, Manitoba. When he was fifteen his family moved to Houston, Texas. When he was nineteen he returned to Vancouver, where he received his BA and MA in English Literature from Simon Fraser University. During the many years that he worked in the post office he published essays and reviews in journals ranging from *The Vancouver Postal Worker* to *The Globe and Mail.* From 1990 to 1997 he published and edited *The Vancouver Review. Colin's Big Thing* is his first book.